Touring
New England
by Bicycle

🚲🚲🚲

Peter Powers

Eugene, Oregon

For Dollie,
whose love and support we appreciate.

Acknowledgements

The routes selected for this book were suggested by three people with many years experience in touring New England by bicycle. Our thanks to John McKeon of New England Bicycle Tours for the Vermont and Cape Islands routes, and to Dennis and Ellen Curran of Maine Coast Cyclers for the Maine routes. Thanks also to our friend Lynne Gately for her hospitality and friendship.

Edited by Melissa Carlson

Cover photo by James Blank /West Stock

TERRAGRAPHICS
P.O. Box 1025
Eugene, Oregon 97440
(503) 343-7115

Manufactured in the United States of America
First Printing, 1991
1   2   3   4   5   6   7   8   9   0

Contents

(cont.)

Introduction

What is your image of summertime New England ? Perhaps it's a small fishing village on a rocky and rugged coastline. Or is it a sweeping beach basking under a hot sun and an ocean begging to cool you off? Maybe you think of picturesque villages with a town green and white church nestled beneath a lush green hillside. You might envision rolling hills of productive farmland, dotted with Holstein cows, red barns and white farmhouses. New England is special because it is all of these – a region of amazing beauty and diversity.

Since there's far more to New England than we can cover in one book, we have tried to present a selection of rides that will be of interest to a variety of cyclists. These routes were recommended by John McKeon of New England Bicycle Tours and Dennis and Ellen Curran of Maine Coast Cyclers. Among them they have many years of leading bicycle tours in the region and they constantly strive to discover the most scenic backroads that are suitable for a cycling vacation.

There is a great deal of variety in the areas covered by the routes in this book. The topography ranges from nearly flat, to rolling hills, to downright steep, and you'll find that every area has some of each. The physical and cultural landscape of these areas varies considerably, too. They all have at least two things in common, however – they are all rural, and not one of them is uninteresting!

Another especially attractive feature of the areas we have chosen is their long tradition of hospitality to visitors. New England country inns and Bed and Breakfast accommodations range from elegant to rustic, and many are well known for their charm and setting. And you'll find excellent restaurants in some of the smallest villages, along with galleries and shops that you might expect to find only in much larger towns. There are opportunities for camping on most of the rides, though some require a modification in the route profiled. A combination of camping and lodging can bring both affordability and a sense of luxury to a several day bike trip.

The focus of this book is its set of maps and profiles. They are as complete as they are unique. Touring, whether by foot or bicycle, puts you into an intimate relationship with the topography of a chosen route. Hills can become mountains and grades can seem to go on forever when you are under your own power. What looks like a winding country road on a typical map may actually be a series of switchbacks that climb up and over yet another ridge separating you from your destination! The 3D maps developed for this book provide you with a true representation of the landscape. The route log and route profile complete the picture of the ride ahead. They won't make it any easier to grind up and over those hills, but they will definitely take some of the unknown, and worry, out of your trip.

Along with the maps in this book, you'll find some general information pertinent to bicycle touring and outdoor activities in this area. Other books cover any one of these topics in great detail. Fitness is especially important to learn about, with an emphasis on developing a good understanding of your capabilities and needs. Touring should be fun and fulfilling – not an unpleasant chore!

This book was designed to be taken with you as you venture into the New England countryside. The compact size is manageable for pocket or pack, and the layout will facilitate the navigation of each route.

Happy touring!

Pete Powers

Route consultants: Dennis Curran, Ellen Curran, and John McKeon

8

Using this Book

The addition of the third dimension to the maps in this book sets them apart from other recreation maps. The computer generated view of the earth's surface provides valuable and clear information about the topography of an area you are planning to tour on bicycle. These 3D views accurately portray the nature of the landscape and the road system that covers it. Combined with the road map, route profile, route log, and description, they provide you with a complete picture of the routes you choose for your New England cycling vacation.

The area mapped

A good portion of central and southern Vermont, a section of the Maine coast, and Massachusetts' Cape Islands are covered by the maps in this book. The 40 routes that are profiled are either one-day loop trips, or one-day sections of multiple day loops. They include a wide range of lengths and topography, providing the opportunity for everyone to pick a route for their ability and interest.

About the maps

While the entire book presents options for trips that span several days, the individual maps can, of course, be used to design a tour that meets your own time and ability constraints. Each map highlights two ways to navigate around a specific area. Use of the profile to evaluate hilliness and length of a route allows you to estimate how long it will take to complete it. The 3D map and road map provide the information you need to pick an alternate route, or perhaps to shorten the one profiled.

The road maps are all oriented with north straight up, while the 3D maps rotate north to get the most complete view of the routes. Be aware that the scale of each map varies depending on the extent of the area being displayed.

(continued on page 12)

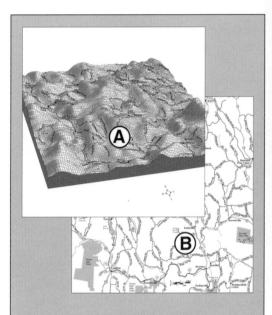

Map elements

(A) 3D map. This map shows the topography of the area and highlights the selected route. It includes most of the roads and features shown on the road map, and will help you select alternate bike routes.

(B) Road map. This is the traditional "planimetric" map showing the route and significant roads, towns, water, geographic features, and map symbols. The mileposts along the route, as well as "direction of travel" arrows, are shown. Some inset maps are included on these pages.

(C) Route profile. This provides a cross-sectional view of each route. Elevation lines are labeled on the left side, and mileage references are indicated along the bottom. Identifiable features are located along the route to help you see where you are.

STOWE TO WATERBURY

Short Route (11.6 miles)

0   Start in downtown Stowe; head south on Rt. 100.
2.6   Intersection with Moscow Rd.
6.9   Turn left at bottom of quick downhill where signs point to Waterbury Center, Loomis Hill, Barnshill.
7.2   Turn right on Guptil Rd.; entering Waterbury Center.
Note: For a dip in Waterbury Reservoir; head du...ward Rt. 100. Turn right on Rt. ...ight on Rt. 100, then immed... ...e reservoir. Cost $1.50.
9.2   Turn ... 100.
9.6   Ben an... ...e Cream Factory on the right; tou... ...ailable.
10.8   Turn left just before I-89 interchange.
11.1   Cross under I-89.
11.6   End at the intersection with South Main St. (Rt. 2) in Waterbury.

Long Route (39.7miles)

0   Start in downtown Stowe: follow short route directions to Waterbury Center.
11.6   Turn right on South Main St. (Rt. 2) in Waterbury.
14.1   Great view of Camel's Hump to the left.
21.7   Jonesville.
25.3   Turn left at traffic light in Richmond;
25.7   Cross over an iron bridge.
25.9   Round Church on the left; nice spot for a rest.
26.0   Turn left after the Church.
26.4   Cemetery on the right.
29.1   Turn left at the 'Y'.
Note: For a swim in Huntington Gorge ladd 3 miles) turn right at the 'Y' up the dirt road with "Cars parked in travelled section of roadway will be towed' sign. Continue past Pendergast Morgan Horse Farm. Look for cliffs and a deep chasm on your left. Use the pull-out above the gorge where the stream is only 10 feet below; the road- it's the most accessible and best swimming hole!
29.3   Road bends left at a red barn.
29.5   Cross an iron bridge over the Winooski River.
29.6   Turn right on Rt. 2.
39.7   End at the traffic light in Waterbury.

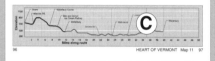

96   HEART OF VERMONT Map 11   97

ⒹRoute logs. This is a complete set of directions for navigating through each route. It is especially useful in weaving your way through urban areas. Each log shows the accumulated distance travelled between turns and identifiable intersections and landmarks.

Index map. *(Title page of each set of maps for a region).* This small map locates the area covered by the larger maps on the following pages.

Area description. *(Title and end page of each set of maps for a region).* This is a general description of the area covered by the single or multiple day rides being profiled.

The route profiles are displayed in a way that lets you easily compare them to each other. Don't be alarmed that some of them look more like a trip across the Himalaya mountains than New England topography – the vertical scale is exaggerated so that more of the "up and down" detail shows. Your first couple of rides will let your eyes and legs reach an understanding of how steep those hills really are!

There are two sets of profiles – with different exaggeration along the vertical axis. The profiles for the Maine and Cape Islands routes, which are quite flat compared to those in Vermont, are set against a blue background, and have a greater exaggeration in elevation. This brings out the small changes in topography that would be lost if they were displayed with the same vertical scale as the routes that venture into the Green Mountains.

Liability disclaimer

Resources

In addition to the highway maps usually available at gas stations and book stores, the following resources may be useful in planning your cycling vacation. All the routes in this book are located in rural settings, and, especially in Vermont, roads are typically not signed on the ground. If you are going to do some exploring on roads other than well-marked highways, you might pick up a reference that does show all the roads in an area, and which indicates the type of surface you can expect to find.

Maps

1. *Specific to bicycling.*

   Bicycle Touring in Vermont. Green Mountain Maps and Guides. *Statewide map showing day loop trips.*

   Summer Recreation Map and Guide for the Mt. Mansfield Region of Vermont. Huntington Graphics. *Has information for cycling and other recreation activities in the Stowe area.*

2. *General road maps and atlases.*

   Vermont Road Atlas and Guide. Northern Cartographic. *Shows roads and road names, towns, lakes, etc. Does not show road surface type. Has information about other recreation opportunities, covered bridges, places of interest, camping, and State Parks.*

   Vermont Atlas and Gazetteer. DeLorme Mapping Co. *Shows roads, road surface type, towns, lakes, etc. Does not show road names. Has information about recreation opportunities, covered bridges, places of interest, geology, camping, and State Parks.*

   Maine Atlas and Gazetteer. DeLorme Mapping Co. *Similar to the Vermont Atlas and Gazetteer.*

Vermont General Highway Map. Vermont Agency of Transportation, Planning Division. *Large scale road maps showing all roads and surface types. No road names. Same information is on the DeLorme Atlas. Has inset maps of the smaller villages.*

3. *Topographic maps.*
United States Geological Survey (USGS).
• 1:100,000 scale series. *Shows roads, towns, lakes, geographic features. Does not show road surface type or road names. Incomplete contour lines for Maine Area. (One inch equals about 1.6 miles.)*
• 1:24,000 scale series. *Shows roads, towns, lakes, features, etc. Shows road surface type and sometimes road names. Incomplete for areas of Maine and Vermont. (One inch equals 2,000 ft.)*

Books

1. *Cycling Guides.*
25 Mountain Bike Tours in Vermont. Backcountry Publications. *25 loop trips throughout the state.*
Vermont Mountain Biking. Acorn Publishing. *25 loop trips in southern Vermont.*
25 Bicycle Tours in Vermont. Backcountry Publications.

2. *General Travel Guide.*
Vermont, an explorers guide. The Countryman Press. *A general guide describing things to do, places to stay and eat, bits of history, etc.*

3. *Cycling Information.*
Anybody's Bike Book. Ten Speed Press. *A repair manual for do-it-yourselfers.*
The Bike Bag Book. Ten Speed Press. *Handlebar bag size version of Anybody's Bike Book. A manual for emergency roadside repairs.*
Bike Touring: The Sierra Club Guide to Outings on Two Wheels. Sierra Club Books. *Complete reference on bicycle equipment and touring gear.*
The Bicycle Touring Book: The Complete Guide to Bicycle Recreation. Rodale Press. *Another comprehensive guide to bicycle touring.*

General Information

1. *Vermont.*
   Vermont Travel Division
   134 State St.
   Montpelier, VT 05602
   (802) 828-3236
   New England Vacation Center
   630 Fifth Ave.
   Concourse Level, Shop #2
   New York, NY 10111
   (212) 307-5780
   Vermont Agency of Natural Resources
   Dept. of Forests, Parks, and Recreation
   Waterbury, VT 05676
   (802) 244-8711
   Green Mountain National Forest
   Federal Building
   151 West St.
   Rutland, VT 05701
   (802) 773-0300

2. *Maine.*
   Maine State Tourism
   Augusta, ME 04333
   (207) 289-5710
   Maine State Parks & Recreation
   Statehouse Station #2
   Augusta, ME 04333
   (207) 289-3821

3. *Massachusetts.*
   Massachusetts Office of Travel & Tourism
   100 Cambridge St., 13th Floor
   Boston, MA 02202
   (617) 727-3201
   Massachusetts Office of Forest & Parks
   100 Cambridge St., 19th Floor
   Boston, MA 02202
   (617) 727-3180 X486

Ferries

1. *Vermont (Lake Champlain).*
   Ferry routes:
   Grand Isle, VT to Plattsburgh, NY,
   Burlington, VT to Port Kent, NY,
   Charlotte, VT to Essex, NY.
   Rate and schedule information:
   Lake Champlain Transportation Co.
   King St. Dock
   Burlington, VT, 05401
   (802) 864-9804.

2. *Maine.*
   Ferry routes:
   Lincolnville to Isleboro. *Year round service, 25 minutes crossing time. 9 ferries each day. $2.00 per person, $4.50 per bicycle.*
   Rockland to North Haven. *Year round service. 1 hour and10 mins. crossing time. 3 ferries each day from end of April to end of Oct. $4.25 per person, $5.50 per bicycle.*
   Rate and schedule information:
   Maine State Ferry Service
   Box 645
   Rockland, ME 04841
   (207) 596-2202.

3. *Massachusetts (Cape Islands).*
   Ferry route:
   Woods Hole to Vineyard Haven/ Oak Bluffs. *Mid-May to mid-Sept. 45 minutes crossing time. 10 ferries each day. $4.50 per person, $2.75 per bicycle.*
   Rate and schedule information:
   Steamship Authority
   Box 284
   Woods Hole, MA 02543
   (508) 540-2022.
   Ferry route:
   Martha's Vineyard to Nantucket. *Mid-June to mid-Sept. 2 hours and 15 minutes crossing time. 3 ferries each day. $10.50 per person, $4.50 per bicycle.*
   Hyannis to Nantucket. *Mid-May to end of Oct. 1 hour and 50 minutes crossing time. 3 ferries each day. $10.50 per person, $4.50 per bicycle.*
   Rate and schedule information:
   Hy-Line Cruises
   Ocean St. Dock
   Hyannis, MA 02601
   (508) 778-2600.

Map Legend

Route 1 (also Route 2 where they coincide). *Corresponding route name and profile are also displayed in blue.*

Milepost for route 1.

Route 2 (where it deviates from Route 1). *Corresponding route name and profile are also displayed in gray.*

Milepost for route 2.

Milepost marking when both routes coincide.

Direction of travel around route. Black arrow indicates direction of travel for both routes when they coincide.

Freeway.

Hard surface road (paved).

All weather surface roads (not paved).

> *Note: Road surface types are not differentiated on Maine maps.*

Ferry route.

Water or lake.

Creek or river.

Parks.

Starting point for each ride.

(continued on next page)

Addison	Small town or community.
Middlebury	Larger town or city.
▲[J]	Public campground. *Letter in box corresponds to listing in the Around New England chapter (pages 161 to 168).*
▲[B]	Privately operated campground. *Letter in box corresponds to listing in the Around New England chapter (pages 161 to 168).*

Map Scale

The scale of each map varies according to the amount of land covered. Refer to the scale bar to estimate distances on the road map. The 3D map is presented in perspective view; i.e., the scale gets smaller from front to back. The route profiles are displayed in a common scale in order to allow easier comparisons among all routes in the book.

Map Orientation

Each of the road maps is oriented with north pointing towards the top of the page. The 3D maps are presented from either a southeast or southwest point of view. The north arrow on each map indicates its orientation. The 3D maps are rotated and scaled to provide the best possible view of the routes being profiled, along with some of the surrounding terrain.

Map Sources

The topography and geographic information contained in the maps in this book are based on USGS 1:100,000 and 1:24,000 series maps, and also on the State of Vermont, Agency of Transportation, 1:63360 series maps.

Road names for the Vermont maps are based on the *Vermont Road Atlas and Guide* published by Northern Cartographic.

New England Index Map

New England is one of the country's best destination areas for a cycling vacation. The maps and information in this book will help you select areas to tour that will match your ability and interests. On the next two pages an index map presents an overview of the areas covered by the more detailed maps that follow. Pages 22 and 23 bring all the route profiles together to give you a quick way to compare their relative hilliness. On page 23, you'll find a summary of all the routes with their mileages and location in the book.

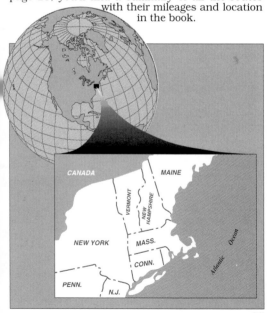

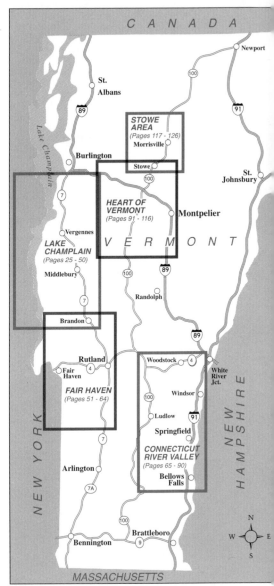

CANADA

Newport

St. Albans

89

Lake Champlain

Burlington

STOWE AREA
(Pages 117 - 126)

Morrisville

Stowe

100

St. Johnsbury

91

7

HEART OF VERMONT
(Pages 91 - 116)

Montpelier

Vergennes

LAKE CHAMPLAIN
(Pages 25 - 50)

V E R M O N T

Middlebury

100

89

Randolph

Brandon

89

Rutland

Woodstock

4

White River Jct.

Fair Haven

4

FAIR HAVEN
(Pages 51 - 64)

Windsor

100

91

Ludlow

7

Springfield

CONNECTICUT RIVER VALLEY
(Pages 65 - 90)

N E W   H A M P S H I R E

N E W   Y O R K

Arlington

7A

Bellows Falls

100

Brattleboro

9

Bennington

MASSACHUSETTS

N
W   E
S

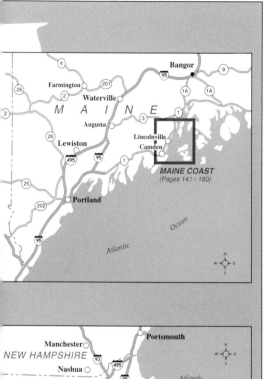

Bangor

Farmington
Waterville

M A I N E

Augusta

Lincolnville
Camden

MAINE COAST
(Pages 141 - 160)

Lewiston

Portland

Ocean

Atlantic

Manchester
NEW HAMPSHIRE
Nashua

Portsmouth

Atlantic

MASSACHUSETTS

Worcester

Boston

Ocean

Providence

RHODE
ISLAND

CONNECTICUT

Hyannis

New
London

**CAPE
ISLANDS**
(Pages 127 - 140)

Nantucket
Island

Martha's
Vineyard

Route Profile Comparison

Lake Champlain (pages 25-50)

Fair Haven (pages 51-64)

Connecticut River Valley (pages 65-90)

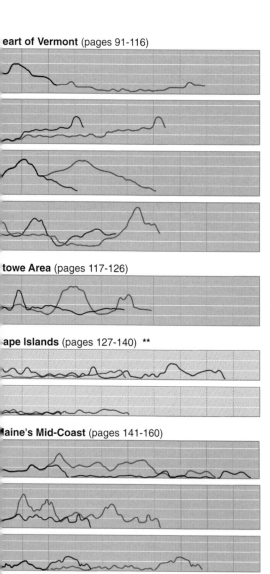

eart of Vermont (pages 91-116)

towe Area (pages 117-126)

ape Islands (pages 127-140) ******

aine's Mid-Coast (pages 141-160)

* Vertical exageration on the Cape Islands profiles are wice that on the other profiles.

Route Summary

Lake Champlain

One of the features of the Lake Champlain valley that appeals to many cyclists is its relatively flat terrain. Gentle hills separate meandering streams and an occasional swamp. The Green Mountains dominate the view to the east, while Lake Champlain and New York's Adirondack Mountains define the western landscape.

The gently rolling valley floor is laced with country roads, many of them paved, and the opportunities for exploring beyond the profiled routes are endless. We describe four days worth of riding, with the routes criss-crossing the valley in several directions. The routes *(continued on page 50)*

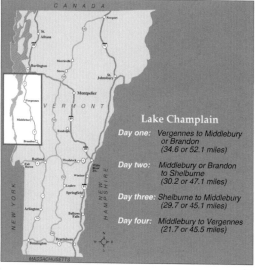

Lake Champlain

Day one: Vergennes to Middlebury or Brandon
(34.6 or 52.1 miles)

Day two: Middlebury or Brandon to Shelburne
(30.2 or 47.1 miles)

Day three: Shelburne to Middlebury
(29.7 or 45.1 miles)

Day four: Middlebury to Vergennes
(21.7 or 45.5 miles)

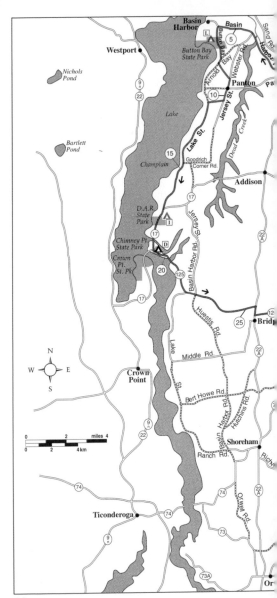

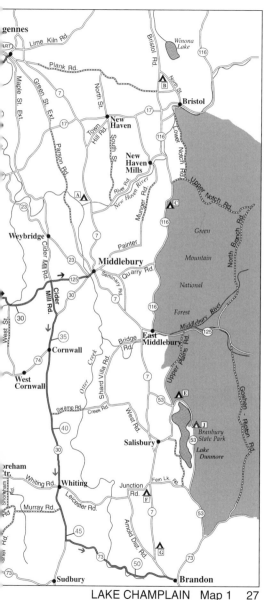

LAKE CHAMPLAIN Map 1 27

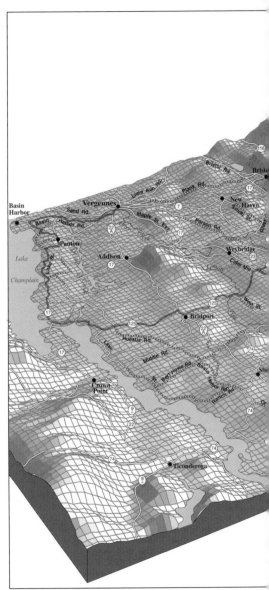

Basin
Harbor

Lake
Champlain

Vergennes

Panton

Addison

Basin Harbor Rd.

Sand Rd.

Lime Kiln Rd.

Plank Rd.

Bristol Rd.

Bristo

New
Haven

South St.

Maple St. Ext.

Parson Rd.

Weybridge

Cider Mill

West St.

Bridport

Huestis Rd.

Middle Rd.

Ben Howe Rd.

Basin Harbor Rd.

Ranch Rd.

Crown
Point

Ticonderoga

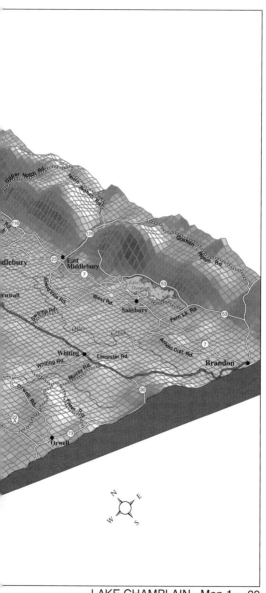

Upper Notch Rd.

North Branch Rd.

Rd. 116

125

Goshen Ripton Rd.

dlebury 23 East Middlebury

7

Shard Villa Rd.

Lake Dunmore 53

rnwall West Rd. Salisbury Fern Lk. Rd. 53

Swamp Rd. Otter Creek

Arnold Dist. Rd. 7

Whiting Leicester Rd. Branden

Whiting Rd. Murray Rd.

Orwell Rd. 30

22 River Rd.

7 Orwell 73

N
E
W
S

VERGENNES TO MIDDLEBURY

34.6 miles

0	Start at the town square in Vergennes; head southwest on Main St. (Rt. 22A South).
0.2	Cross Otter Creek.
0.5	**Turn right on Panton Rd.**
1.9	**Turn right on Basin Harbor Rd.**
6.4	**Turn left on Button Bay Rd.** (follow sign to Button Bay State Park).
7.1	Entrance to Button Bay State Park (camping, picnicking, and swimming).
9.2	**Turn right at 'Y' at bottom of hill.**
9.6	Straight onto Webster Rd. (Sand Rd.) at Burnett's Store; becomes Jersey St.
10.2	**Bear right at bend onto Pease Rd.;** becomes Lake St.
13.8	Yankee Kingdom Store and Orchards.
17.0	Continue straight onto Rt. 17 toward Chimney Point.
19.0	Bridge to N.Y.; **bear left onto Rt. 125.**
22.8	Intersection with Basin Harbor Rd.
25.4	**Turn right on Rt. 22A.**
25.9	**Turn left on Rt. 125 toward Middlebury.**
32.3	Intersection with Cider Mill Rd.
34.6	End in Middlebury at the town square.

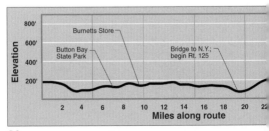

VERGENNES TO BRANDON

52.1 miles

0	Start at the town square in Vergennes; head southwest on Main St. (Rt. 22A South).
.2	Cross Otter Creek.
.5	**Turn right on Panton Rd.**
1.9	**Turn right on Basin Harbor Rd.**
5.4	**Turn left on Button Bay Rd.** (follow sign to Button Bay State Park).
7.1	Entrance to Button Bay State Park (camping, picnicking, and swimming).
9.2	**Turn right at 'Y' at bottom of hill.**
9.6	Straight onto Webster Rd. (Sand Rd.) at Burnett's Store; becomes Jersey St.
10.2	**Bear right at bend onto Pease Rd.;** becomes Lake St.
13.8	Yankee Kingdom Store and Orchards.
17.0	Continue straight onto Rt. 17 toward Chimney Point.
19.0	Bridge to N.Y.; **bear left onto Rt. 125.**
22.8	Intersection with Basin Harbor Rd.
25.4	**Turn right on Rt. 22A.**
25.9	**Turn left on Rt. 125 toward Middlebury.**
32.3	**Turn right on Cider Mill Rd.** (watch for blinking light).
34.1	**Turn right on Rt. 30.**
35.5	Cornwall.
43.2	Whiting.
45.2	**Turn left on Rt. 73.**
52.1	End at the town green in Brandon.

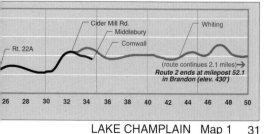

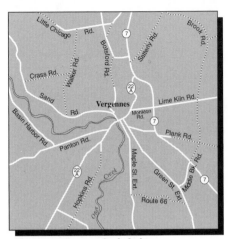

Vergennes and vicinity

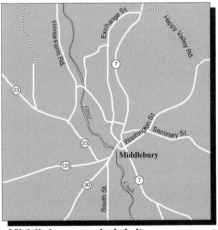

Middlebury and vicinity

Note: *Because this map covers such a large area, you'll find more detail on the other maps covering this region.*

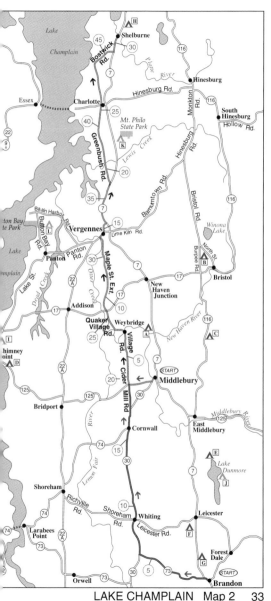

LAKE CHAMPLAIN   Map 2   33

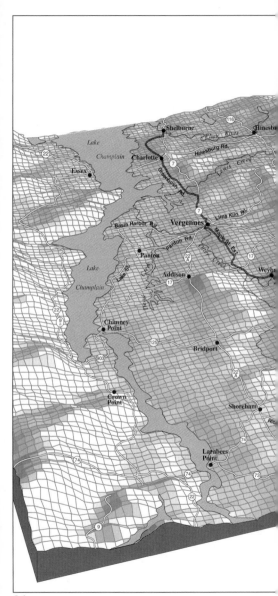

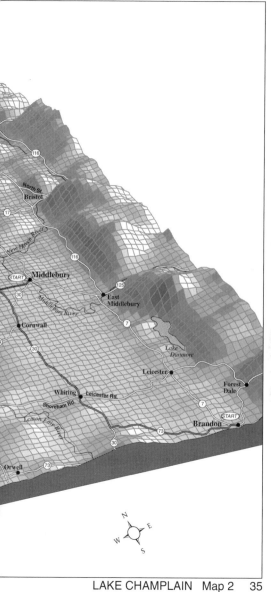

116

North St
Bristol

17

New Haven River

116

START Middlebury

30

Middlebury River

125

East
Middlebury

7

Cornwall

30

Lake
Dunmore

Leicester

Forest
Dale

Whiting   Leicester Rd.

7

Shoreham Rd.

START

Lemon Fair River

Brandon

30

73

Orwell

73

N
W — E
S

MIDDLEBURY TO SHELBURNE

30.2 miles

0   Start at the town square in Middlebury; head
west on Rt. 125.

2.3   Turn right on Cider Mill Rd.

4.6   Intersection with Rt. 23; continue straight
onto Village Rd.

6.4   Weybridge Dam.

8.8   Intersection with Rt. 17; continue straight
onto Hallock Rd.

14.8   Turn right on Main St. (Rt. 22A).

14.9   Vergennes town center; continue straight
on Rt. 22A.

16.1   Turn left on Rt. 7.

19.1   Rokeby Museum on right.

19.2   Turn left on Greenbush Rd. (unmarked).

21.5   Intersection with Stage Rd. (on right).

**23.4   Continue straight, then right, through
intersection with Thompson's Point Rd.**
(at the top of a small hill - dirt road
on right).

25.6   Intersection with Ferry Rd. (Hinesburg Rd.);
Williams Brick Store on corner.

27.3   Cross under RR tressle.

**29.5   Turn left on Rt. 7; Shelburne Museum
on left.**

30.2   End in Shelburne.

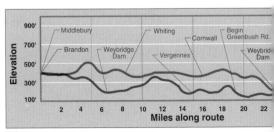

BRANDON TO SHELBURNE

47.1 miles

0   Start at the town green in Brandon; head north on Rt. 7.

0.3   Turn left on Rt. 73.

6.3   Turn right on Rt. 30 (big red farm on the corner).

8.3   Whiting.

16.0 Cornwall.

17.4 Turn left on Cider Mill Rd. where Rt. 30 bends to right and Ridge Rd. goes to left.

19.2 Intersection with Rt. 125; continue straight.

21.5 Intersection with Rt. 23; continue straight onto Village Rd.

23.3 Weybridge Dam.

25.7 Intersection with Rt. 17; continue straight onto Hallock Rd.

31.7 Turn right on Main St. (Rt. 22A).

31.8 Vergennes town center; continue straight on Rt. 22A.

33.0 Turn left on Rt. 7.

36.0 Rokeby Museum on right.

36.1 Turn left on Greenbush Rd. (unmarked).

38.4 Intersection with Stage Rd. (on right).

40.3 Continue straight, then right, through intersection with Thompson's Point Rd. (at the top of a small hill - dirt road on right).

42.5 Intersection with Ferry Rd. (Hinesburg Rd.); Williams Brick Store on corner.

44.2 Cross under RR tressle.

46.4 Turn left on Rt. 7; Shelburne Museum on left.

47.1 End in Shelburne.

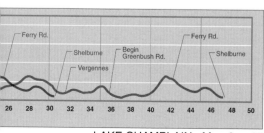

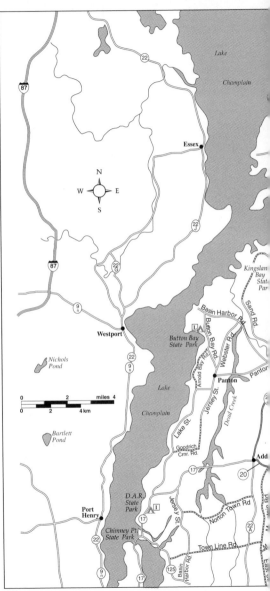

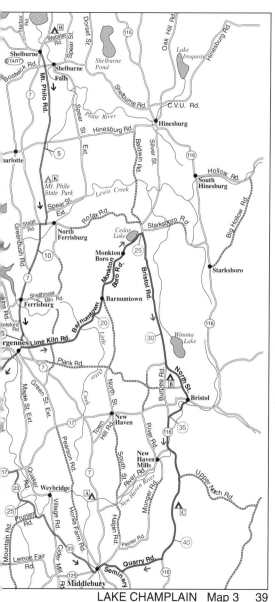

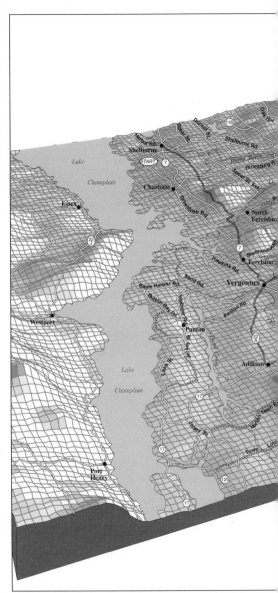

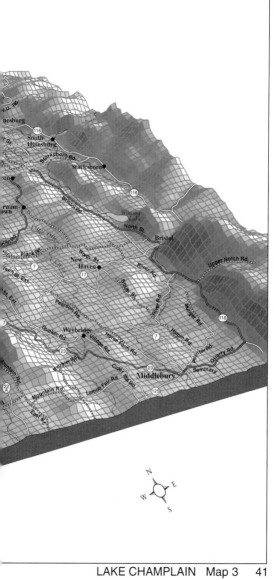

nesburg

South
Hinesburg

116

Starksboro

Starksboro Rd.

on

116

Bristol Rd.

Winona
Lake

North St.

rnum-
wn

Bristol

Plank Rd.

North St.

New
Haven

17

River Rd.

Upper Notch Rd.

reen St. Ext.

7

Pearson Rd.

South St.

Baker Rd.

Munger Rd.

116

St. Ext.

7

Quaker Rd.

Weybridge

Village Rd.

Horse Farm Rd.

Halpin Rd.

7

Painter Rd.

Quarry Rd.

ountain Rd.

23

Sheller Rd.

Cider Mill Rd.

23

Middlebury

Seminary

Mountain Rd.

Lemon Fair Rd.

125

Egan St.

SHELBURNE TO MIDDLEBURY

Short Route (29.7 miles)

0	Start at the town in Shelburne; head south on Falls Rd.
0.7	Intersection with Marsett Rd.
4.6	Continue straight through blinking light onto Mt. Philo Rd.
8.7	**Turn right on Hollow Rd. at 'T' intersection.**
9.0	**Turn left on Rt. 7.**
14.5	**Turn right on Rt. 22A to Vergennes.**
15.6	Town of Vergennes; continue through town on Rt. 22A.
19.7	**Turn left on Rt. 17 in Addison.**
23.7	**Turn right on Rt. 23 just before a small bridge.**
28.6	**Bear left onto Rt. 125.**
29.5	**Bear left on Rt. 30.**
29.7	End at the town green in Middlebury.

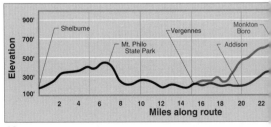

Long Route (45.1 miles)

0   Start at the town green in Shelburne; head
         south on Falls Rd.

0.7   Intersection with Marsett Rd.

4.6   Continue straight through blinking light
         onto Mt. Philo Rd.

**8.7   Turn right on Hollow Rd. at 'T'
         intersection.**

9.0   Turn left on Rt. 7.

14.5   Turn right on Rt. 22A to Vergennes.

15.5   Turn left on Monkton Rd.

16.0   Intersection with Rt. 7; continue straight
         onto Lime Kiln Rd.

23.4   Monkton Boro.

25.0   Turn right on Bristol Rd.

**31.8   Bear left onto North St. towards Bristol
         just after Hardscrabble Rd.**

33.8   Bristol Village; continue straight across
         Rt. 17 onto South St.

**34.4   Turn right on Hewitt Rd.; cross bridge
         over New Haven River.**

35.2   Turn left on Rt. 116.

41.2   Turn right on Quarry Rd.

43.6   Bear right on Seminary St. Ext.

44.8   Turn left on Washington St.

45.1   End at the town square in Middlebury.

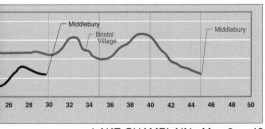

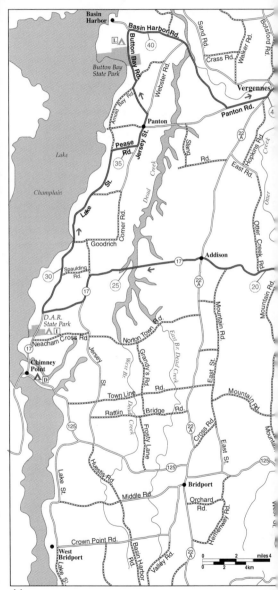

Basin
Harbor
Basin Harbor Rd.
Sand Rd.
Botsford Rd.
Walker Rd.
Crass Rd.
L
40
Button Bay Rd.
Webster Rd.
Button Bay
State Park
Arnold Bay Rd.
Vergennes
4
Panton Rd.
Panton Rd.
Panton
22A
Pease Rd.
Jersey St.
Slang Rd.
Hopkins Rd.
East Rd.
Lake
Champlain
Lake
35
Lake St.
Dead Creek
Otter Creek
Corner Rd.
Goodrich
30
Spaulding Rd.
17
25
Addison
17
22A
20
Otter Creek Rd.
Mountain Rd.
D.A.R.
State Park
I
17
Neacham Cross Rd.
Chimney
Point
D
Jersey St.
Norton Town Rd.
West Br.
East Br. Dead Creek
Grandy's Rd.
Mountain Rd.
East St.
Mountain Rd.
125
Town Line Rd.
Dead Creek
Bridge Rd.
Ratlin
Frosty Lane
22A
Cross Rd.
East St.
Mountain Rd.
125
125
Bridport
Lake St.
Huestis Rd.
Middle Rd.
Orchard Rd.
Hemenway Rd.
West St.
Crown Point Rd.
West
Bridport
Lake St.
Basin Harbor Rd.
Valley Rd.
22A

miles 4
0 2
0 2
4km

44

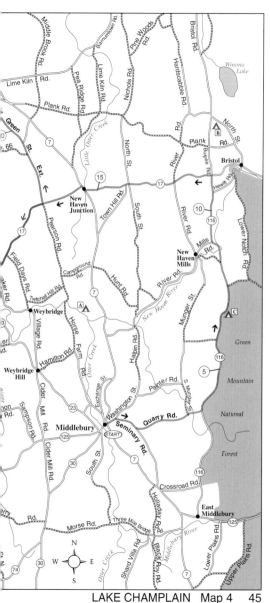

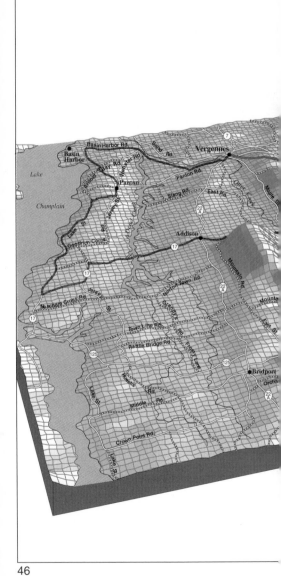

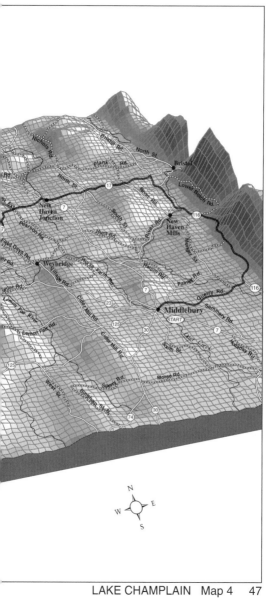

Nichols Rd.

Bristol Rd.

North St.

Plank Rd.

Bristol

North St.

17

Boro Rd.

Lower Notch Rd.

7

New Haven Junction

South St.

116

River Rd.

Roberson Rd.

New Haven Mills

Field Days Rd.

Hum Rd.

Munger St.

Weybridge

Forks Farm Rd.

Village Rd.

Halpin Rd.

Palmer Rd.

Quarry Rd.

7

Cider Mill Rd.

23

Middlebury

Seminary Rd.

START

116

Lemon Fair Rd.

125

Cider Mill Rd.

30

Seth St.

Otter Creek

7

West St.

Spear Rd.

Shoreham St. N.

Morse Rd.

Meadow Rd.

125

74

30

N
W · E
S

MIDDLEBURY TO VERGENNES

Short Route (21.7 miles)

0   Start at the town square in Middlebury; head
       northwest on Washington St.
0.3   Turn right on Seminary St. Ext.
**1.3   Bear left onto Quarry Rd. where Foote St.
       continues straight.**
3.5   Turn left on Rt. 116.
6.6   Elephant Mountain Camping on right.
9.0   Cross narrow bridge over New Haven River.
11.5   Turn left on Rt. 17.
14.4   New Haven; continue straight on Rt. 17.
15.8   Turn right on Rt. 7.
**16.0   Turn left back onto Rt.17 immediately
       after crossing RR tracks.**
17.4   Turn right on Green St. Ext. (not marked).
21.5   Continue straight onto Green St.
21.7   End at the town square in Vergennes.

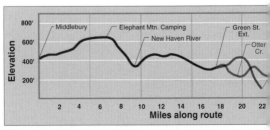

48

Long Route (45.5 miles)

)   Start at the town square in Middlebury; head northwest on Washington St.

0.3 Turn right on Seminary St. Ext.

1.3 Bear left onto Quarry Rd. where Foote St. continues straight.

3.5 Turn left on Rt. 116.

5.6 Elephant Mountain Camping on right.

9.0 Cross narrow bridge over New Haven River.

11.5 Turn left on Rt. 17.

14.4 New Haven; continue straight on Rt. 17.

15.8 Turn right on Rt. 7.

16.0 Turn left back onto Rt.17 immediately after crossing RR tracks.

17.4 Intersection with Green St. Ext.

19.4 Intersection with Hallock Rd.

19.5 Cross bridge over Otter Cr.

19.6 Intersection with Rt. 23.

22.4 Intersection with Rt. 22A.

28.4 Turn right on Lake St.

35.2 Turn left at 'T' intersection on Jersey St.

35.8 Continue straight where main road (Panton Rd.) turns right.

36.2 Turn left at 'Y' intersection on Button Bay Rd. following sign to Button Bay State Park.

38.3 Entrance to Button Bay State Park.

39.1 Turn right on Basin Harbor Rd.

43.6 Turn left on Panton Rd.

45.0 Turn left on Rt. 22A.

45.5 End at the town square in Vergennes.

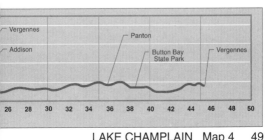

(continued from page 25)

wind along the shoreline of the lake, traverse open farmland, and climb a few ridges in the foothills of the Green Mountain National Forest. A classic New England scene, complete with Holsteins, is often waiting around the next bend in the road throughout this productive farming region.

There are many small villages scattered throughout the valley, and some are more apparent on the map than they are on the ground. Middlebury is the area's main town, and is a good place to treat yourself to a special meal or place to stay. It also would be hard to beat if you are looking for somewhere to base yourself for several one-day loop rides. Besides the many options for riding to the north, south, and west of town, you'll find a good selection of accommodations and restaurants to choose from. Among the small towns, Bristol village stands out as one of the most attractive and is a great spot to plan for a lunch stop.

If you are designing a trip with camping in mind, there are more choices in this region than in other parts of the state, and the terrain is a little more forgiving to a rider with a fully loaded touring bike. Other types of lodging are also found in abundance in the area. High-end and historic Inns, Bed and Breakfast accommodations, motels, and resorts are scattered throughout the towns and countryside.

Overall, the many country roads, the gentle topography, the classic New England farming landscape, and the great food and lodging have long made the Lake Champlain valley a favorite area for cyclists.

Fair Haven

Situated at the southern end of the Lake Champlain valley, the town of Fair Haven is the starting point for the four loop routes described in this section. There is more variety in the topography of this area than there is in the area covered by the Lake Champlain routes just north of here. The rides on the first day cover a gently rolling landscape of interspersed farm and forest lands. On day two you venture into the hills to the east, and into more consistently forested terrain.

Riding north of Fair Haven takes you into an area dotted with many lakes and ponds, the largest of which is Lake Bomoseen. *(continued on page 64)*

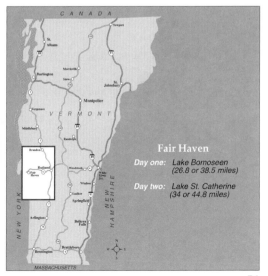

Fair Haven

Day one: Lake Bomoseen
(26.8 or 38.5 miles)

Day two: Lake St. Catherine
(34 or 44.8 miles)

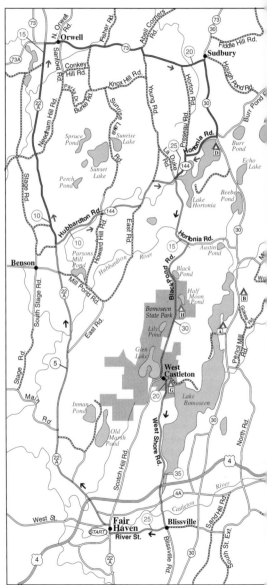

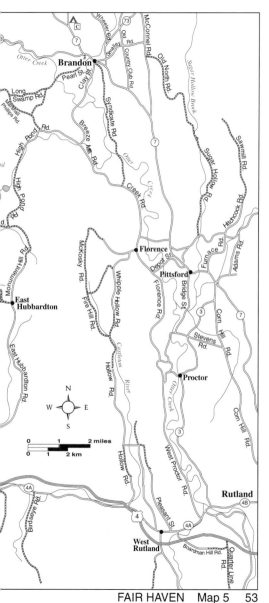

Otter Creek

Brandon

Wheeler Rd.

73

McConnel Rd.

Old Rd.

Shelley

7

Country Club Rd.

Old North Rd.

Sugar Hollow Brook

C

Long Swamp Rd.

Pearl St.

Clay Rd.

Marshall Phillips Rd.

Syndicate Rd.

Breeze Mt. Rd.

High Pond Rd.

7

Otter

Creek

Sugar Hollow Rd.

Sawmill Rd.

High Pond Rd.

Creek Rd.

Creek

Hitchcock Rd.

Monument Hill Rd.

McKosky Rd.

Florence

Depot St.

Pittsford

Furnace Rd.

Adams Rd.

East Hubbardton

Fire Hill Rd.

Whipple Hollow Rd.

Florence Rd.

Bridge St.

3

Corn Hill Rd.

7

East Hubbardton Rd.

Castleton

Hollow Rd.

River

Stevens Rd.

Proctor

Otter Creek

Corn Hill Rd.

N
W — E
S

0 1 2 miles
0 1 2 km

3

West Proctor Rd.

Hollow Rd.

Rutland

4B

4A

Birdseye Rd.

Pleasant St.

4

West Rutland

4A

Boardman Hill Rd.

Quarter Line Rd.

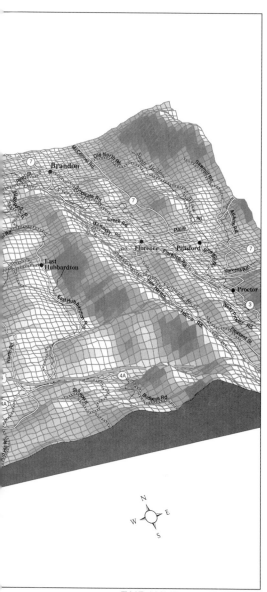

Brandon
East Hubbardton
Florence
Pittsford
Proctor

LAKE BOMOSEEN

Short Route (26.8 miles)

0	Start at the town green in Fair Haven; head north on Rt. 22A.
0.8	Cross under Rt. 4.
4.3	Road narrows - watch for traffic.
5.7	Racetrack on left.
6.0	Intersection with East Rd.
9.5	**Turn right on Rt. 144.**
12.9	**Turn right (almost a 'U' turn) on Hortonia Rd.;** Lake Hortonia General Store is just ahead on Rt. 144.
14.7	**Bear left at fork to stay on paved road.**
15.2	**Turn right on Black Pond Rd.** - look for small sign to Half Moon State Park; road becomes dirt.
16.6	Entrance to Half Moon State Park on left.
19.7	**Bear left at unmarked fork.**
19.8	**Turn left on Scotch Hill Rd. at stop sign.**
19.9	Entrance to Bomoseen State Park on left; swimming and picnicking.
21.3	Lake Bomoseen on left.
23.3	Cross over Rt. 4.
23.8	**Turn left at stop sign (Hydeville Ctr.) on Rt. 4A; cross bridge then immediate right on Blissville Rd.**
24.0	Cross RR tracks.
24.7	**Turn right on River St. at Blissville Ctr.**
26.2	RR overpass.
26.6	**Turn right at stop sign on Rt. 22A in Fair Haven.**
26.8	End at the town green in Fair Haven.

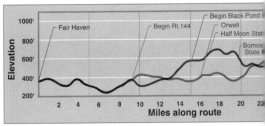

Long Route (38.5 miles)

Start at the town green in Fair Haven; head north on Rt. 22A.

.8 Cross under Rt. 4.

.3 Road narrows - watch for traffic.

.7 Racetrack on left.

.0 Intersection with East Rd.

5.5 Turn right on Rt. 73.

6.0 Orwell.

0.5 Turn right on Rt. 30 where Rt. 73 turns left to Sudbury.

2.5 Turn right on Rt. 144 (Hortonia Rd.).

3.0 Lake Hortonia on left.

4.6 Bear left at fork just after Lake Hortonia General Store.

6.4 Bear left at fork to stay on paved road.

6.9 Turn right on Black Pond Rd. - look for small sign to Half Moon State Park; road becomes dirt.

8.3 Entrance to Half Moon State Park on left.

1.4 Bear left at unmarked fork.

1.5 Turn left on Scotch Hill Rd. at stop sign.

1.6 Entrance to Bomoseen State Park on left; swimming and picnicking.

3.0 Lake Bomoseen on left.

5.0 Cross over Rt. 4.

5.5 Turn left at stop sign (Hydeville Ctr.) on Rt. 4A; cross bridge then immediate right on Blissville Rd.

5.7 Cross RR tracks.

6.4 Turn right on River St. at Blissville Ctr.

7.9 RR overpass.

8.3 Turn right at stop sign on Rt. 22A in Fair Haven.

8.5 End at the town green in Fair Haven.

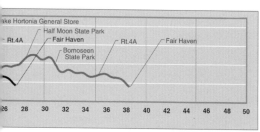

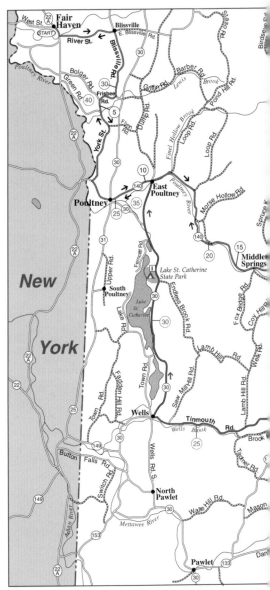

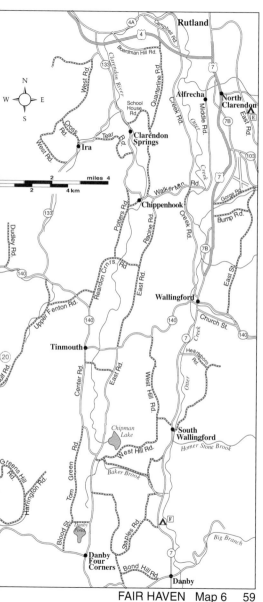

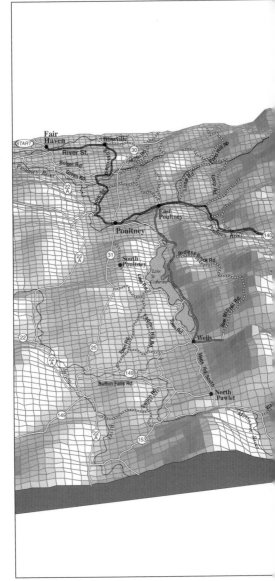

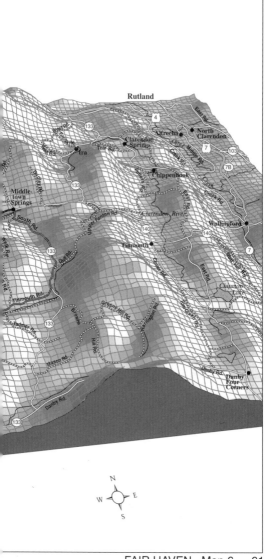

Rutland

Clarendon Springs

Ira

Chippenhook

Middle-town Springs

Clarendon River

Tinmouth

Alfrecha

North Clarendon

Wallingford

Chipman Lake

Danby Four Corners

N
W E
S

LAKE ST. CATHERINE

Short Route (34.0 miles)

0	Start at the town green in Fair Haven; head south on Main St. (Rt. 22A).
0.2	**Turn left on River St.** (first left after leaving town green).
2.1	**Turn right at stop sign on Blissville Rd. at Blissville Center.**
4.1	**Turn right at stop sign on Frisbee;** .5 mile dirt road through slate quarry.
4.8	**Turn left at "T" intersection on Bolger Rd.;** becomes York St.
7.7	**Turn left at stop sign where a right turn would take you across a small bridge into N.Y. State.**
7.9	**Bear right at stop sign.**
8.2	**Turn left on Main St. into Poultney;** entrance to Green Mountain College is on the right.
8.5	Poultney town center; continue straight onto Rt. 140 E. (Horace Greeley Memorial Hwy.).
10.2	East Poultney.
17.0	Middletown Springs; **turn around point.** *Note: To get to the springs take first right past the general store on Rt. 133. The springs are in a small park on the left.*

Retrace route back to Fairhaven.

34.0 End at the town green.

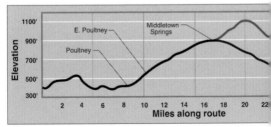

Long Route (44.8 miles)

0 Start at the town green in Fair Haven; head south on Main St. (Rt. 22A).

0.2 Turn left on River St. (first left after leaving town green).

2.1 Turn right at stop sign on Blissville Rd. at Blissville Center.

4.1 Turn right at stop sign on Frisbee; .5 mile dirt road through slate quarry.

4.8 Turn left at "T" intersection on Bolger Rd.; becomes York St.

7.7 Turn left at stop sign where a right turn would take you across a small bridge into N.Y. State.

7.9 Bear right at stop sign.

8.2 Turn left on Main St. into Poultney; entrance to Green Mountain College is on the right.

8.5 Poultney town center; continue straight onto Rt. 140 E. (Horace Greeley Memorial Hwy.).

10.2 East Poultney.

17.0 Turn right on Rt. 133 south in Middletown Springs.

22.2 Turn right on Tinmouth Rd.; look for sign to Wells on left.

23.1 Begin .6 mile stretch of dirt road.

27.2 Wells; bear right onto Rt. 30 at stop sign.

29.0 Lake St. Catherine on left.

31.2 Entrance to Lake St. Catherine State Park on left.

33.2 Bear right on Thrall Rd.; radio station at intersection.

34.6 Cross bridge over gorge and enter E. Poultney; **turn left on Rt. 140.**

Retrace route back to Fair Haven.

44.8 End at the town green.

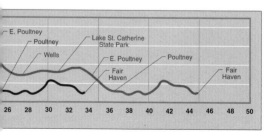

(continued from page 51)

In addition to camping, the State Park on the lake offers a chance for a refreshing swim after a long ride on a hot day. Black Pond Rd., between Hortonia Rd. and West Shore Rd. is unpaved. An alternate route back to Fair Haven is the paved, but more heavily trafficked, Rt. 30.

South of Fair Haven you'll have a chance to test your legs on a more rolling terrain, and be rewarded with the discovery of several classically picturesque Vermont villages. Have your camera ready for East Poultney! The historic Middletown Springs are said to have recuperative powers, and they also provide a nice picnic spot. If you have the energy, you can extend your ride all the way to Pawlet on Rt. 133, returning by way of North Pawlet and Wells.

In addition to these loops north and south of Fair Haven, there is also some excellent riding in the Rutland/Wallingford area. One good day trip into that area starts in Fair Haven, heads east on Rt. 4A, then north on West Proctor Rd. to the Vermont Marble Works in Proctor. You can return the same way or by taking Rt. 3 to connect with Rt. 4A. Wallingford is the starting point for several loops into the Tinmouth area. After climbing a steep hill out of the Otter Creek valley, you'll enjoy the rolling terrain and many small villages characteristic of this part of the state. In addition to the villages encountered along the Fair Haven routes, Wells, Pawlet, and North Pawlet are particularly attractive.

Connecticut River Valley

These routes compose a four-day loop that starts and ends in historic Woodstock. This long established resort town has been attracting visitors for over a century, and is considered one of the prettiest in the country. Most of the village, and the hamlet of South Woodstock on Rt. 106, are on the National Register of Historic Places.

The first two days of the ride are spent in the hills and valleys of Central Vermont. You'll follow several rivers, and climb a few ridges between them, as you head west, then south, to Chester. Forested hillsides present a constant backdrop to valley floors covered with *(continued on page 90)*

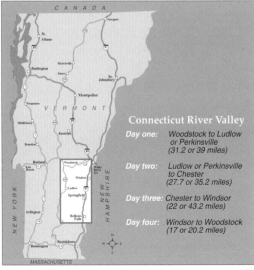

Connecticut River Valley

Day one: Woodstock to Ludlow or Perkinsville (31.2 or 39 miles)

Day two: Ludlow or Perkinsville to Chester (27.7 or 35.2 miles)

Day three: Chester to Windsor (22 or 43.2 miles)

Day four: Windsor to Woodstock (17 or 20.2 miles)

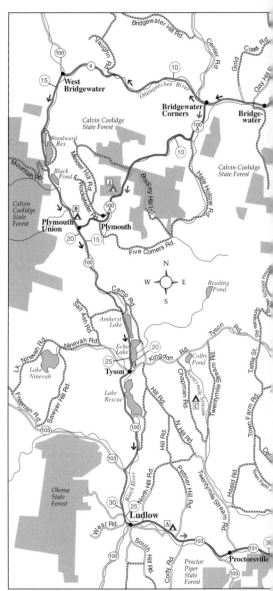

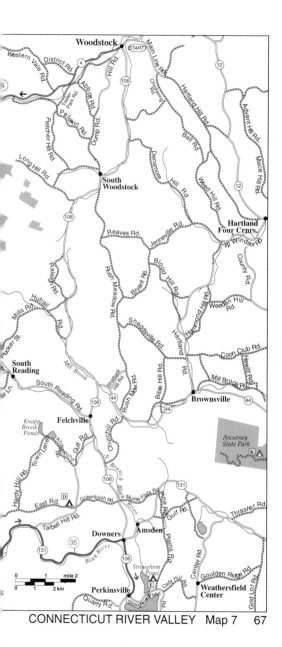

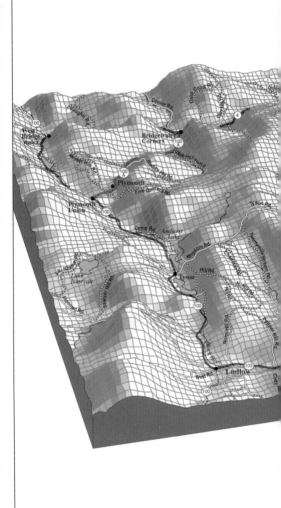

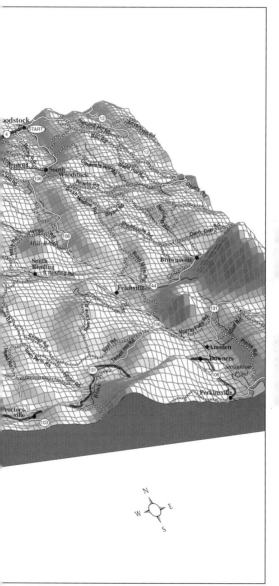

WOODSTOCK TO LUDLOW

31.2 miles

0   Start at the town green in Woodstock; head west on Rt. 4.
0.4   Cross iron bridge with lamps.
1.4   West Woodstock.
6.3   Market Place factory outlet in Bridgewater.
7.0   Recreation area on left.
8.3   Intersection with Rt. 100A at Bridgewater Corners.
14.1 Turn left on Rt. 100.
16.4 Woodward Reservoir; pavement narrows.
19.8 Intersection with Rt. 100A.
24.0 Lake Amherst on left.
24.9 Echo Lake on left.
25.8 Tyson.
26.6 Lake Rescue on left.
27.9 Green Mountain Sugar House on left.
29.4 Turn left to stay on Rt. 100 at intersection with Rt. 103 ('T' intersection).
30.6 Entering Ludlow; travel through village on Main St.; **bear left over bridge with globe lights onto Rt. 103 south.**
31.2 End in downtown Ludlow.

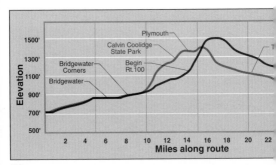

WOODSTOCK TO PERKINSVILLE

39.0 miles

0	Start at the town green in Woodstock; head west on Rt. 4.
0.4	Cross iron bridge with lamps.
1.4	West Woodstock.
6.3	Market Place factory outlet in Bridgewater.
7.0	Recreation area on left.
8.3	**Turn left on Rt. 100A at Bridgewater Corners.**
12.1	Mountain spring on left.
12.7	Coolidge State Park on left.
14.0	Plymouth; President Calvin Coolidge birthplace and Plymouth Cheese Factory on loop road off to right; good picnic and rest area.
14.5	**Turn left on Rt. 100 south.**
18.7	Lake Amherst on left.
19.6	Echo Lake on left.
20.5	Tyson.
21.3	Lake Rescue on left.
22.6	Green Mountain Sugar House on left.
24.1	**Turn left to stay on Rt. 100 at intersection with Rt. 103** (T intersection).
25.3	Entering Ludlow; travel through village on Main St.; **bear left over bridge with globe lights onto Rt. 103 south.**
27.7	Joseph Cerniglia Winery on right; tours available.
28.3	**Turn left on Rt. 131 east into Proctorsville.**
36.5	Covered bridge on right.
36.8	**Turn right on Rt. 106.**
38.5	Intersection with Stroughton Pond Rd. on left. *Note: For a good place to swim, turn left on Stroughton Pond Rd., go 0.7 mile to the Pond.*
39.0	End in Perkinsville.

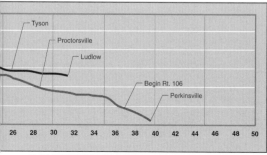

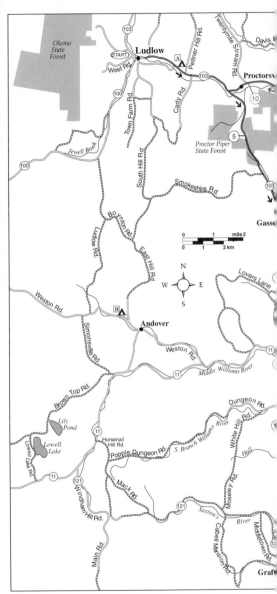

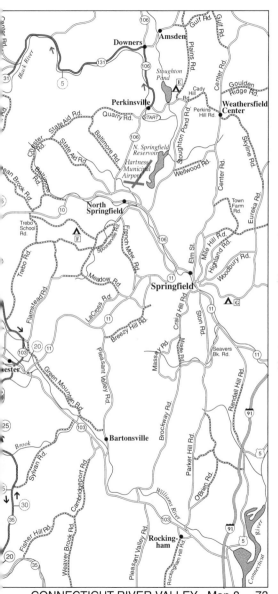

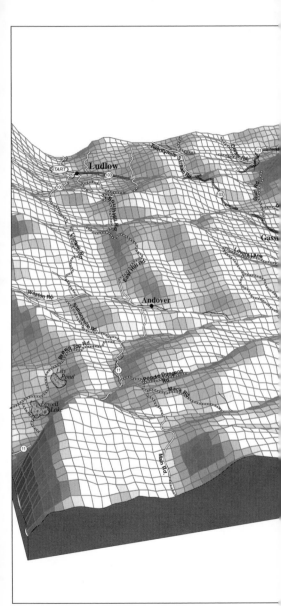

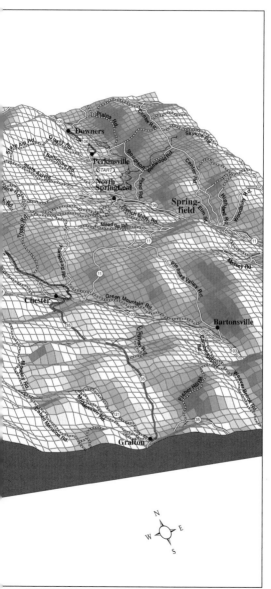

LUDLOW TO CHESTER

27.7 miles

0 Start in downtown Ludlow; head east on Rt. 103.
1.8 Joseph Cerniglia Winery on right; tours available.
3.2 Intersection with Rt. 131 to Proctorsville.
8.1 Intersection with Rt. 10.
11.4 Enter Chester; follow signs for Rt. 103 south and Rt. 11.
12.9 Intersection with Rt. 11; continue south on Rt. 35.
     Note: For a very short option, turn right and end at the town green just ahead.
20.2 Grafton; **turn around point.**
27.5 Turn left on Rt. 11.
27.7 End at the town green in Chester.

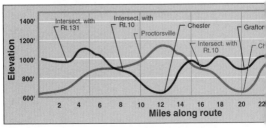

PERKINSVILLE TO CHESTER

35.2 miles

0   Start in Perkinsville; head north on Rt. 106.
2.2   Turn left on Rt. 131.
10.2 Proctorsville.
10.7 Turn left on Rt. 103.
15.6 Intersection with Rt. 10.
18.9 Enter Chester; follow signs for Rt. 103 south
      and Rt. 11.
20.4 Intersection with Rt. 11; continue straight
      onto Rt. 35.
      *Note: For shorter route, turn right and end
      at the town green just ahead.*
27.7 Grafton; **turn around point.**
35.0 Turn left on Rt. 11.
35.2 End at the town green in Chester.

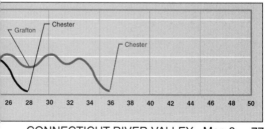

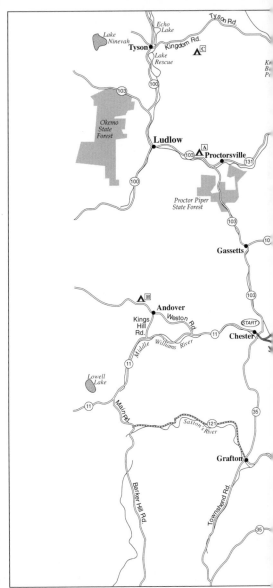

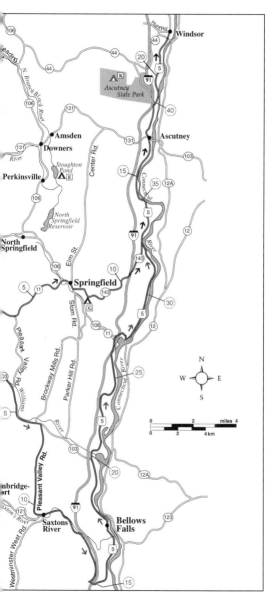

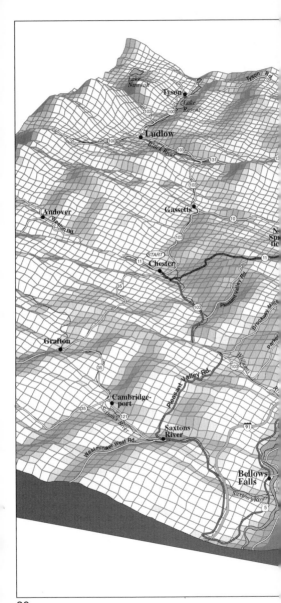

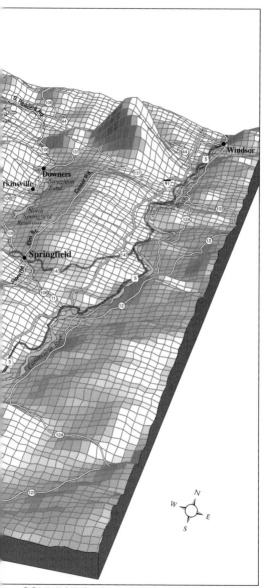

S. Reading Rd

106

44

106   131

131

Center Rd

44

91

Windsor

5

Downers   Stoughton
Pond

rkinsville

100

North
Springfield
Reservoir

106

Elm St

Springfield

143

12A

103

12

143

5

State Rd

106   11

12

5

Connecticut River

12A

125

N
W ⊕ E
S

CHESTER TO WINDSOR

Short Route (22.0 miles)

0	Start at the town green in Chester; head east on Rt. 11.
0.4	**Turn left to stay on Rt. 11.**
6.5	**Turn right on Rt. 106;** Springfield Shopping Plaza on right.
7.1	**Turn left on Rt. 143 in the center of town.**
9.1	**Bear right to stay on Rt. 143.**
9.9	**Bear left at "Y" to stay on Rt. 143.**
10.9	Cross under I-91.
12.3	**Turn left on Rt. 5.**
15.8	Wilgus State Park on right.
17.0	Ascutney; continue straight through lights.
17.7	Carney's Market on left.
22.0	End in downtown Windsor.

*Note: Covered bridge and St. Ganden's option.
Continue straight 0.1 mile, then turn right to
cross the world's longest covered bridge. Go
0.6 miles, then turn left on NH Rte. 12A.
Proceed 1.1 miles and turn right to the St.
Ganden's National Historic Site.
Return to Windsor by same route.*

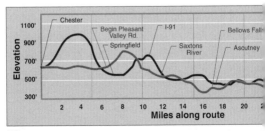

82

Long Route (43.2 miles)

0	Start at the town green in Chester; head east on Rt. 11.
0.4	Continue straight onto Rt. 103.
2.7	Chester Store.
5.6	**Turn right on Pleasant Valley Rd. to Saxtons River;** watch for sign about 20 yards ahead of the turn.
11.0	Recreation area on left.
11.3	**Bear left.**
11.4	**Turn left at stop sign on Rt. 121 east.**
11.8	Saxtons River Village
12.0	Cross over Saxton's River.
13.0	Covered bridge on left.
14.5	Cross under I-91.
16.2	Intersection with Rt. 5; continue straight through light at bottom of hill.
16.7	Miss Bellows Falls diner on left.
17.0	**Bear right onto Rt. 5**
19.8	**Turn right to stay on Rt. 5 north where Rt. 103 continues straight.**
26.5	Cross under I-91.
27.1	**Turn right on Rt. 11.**
27.9	**Turn left to rejoin Rt. 5 north.**
33.5	Intersection with Rt. 143.
37.0	Wilgus State Park.
38.2	Ascutney; continue straight through lights.
38.9	Carney's Market on left.
43.2	End in downtown Windsor.

See note on short route for interesting option.

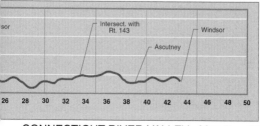

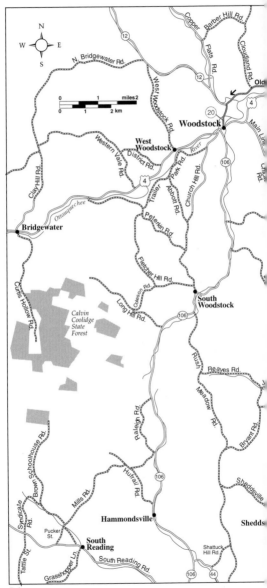

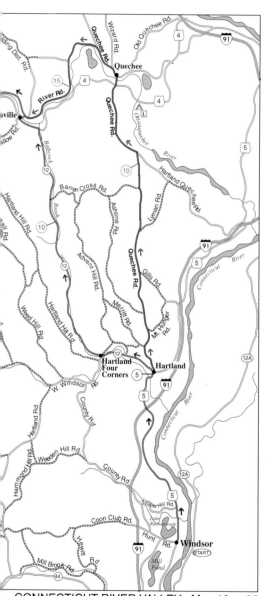

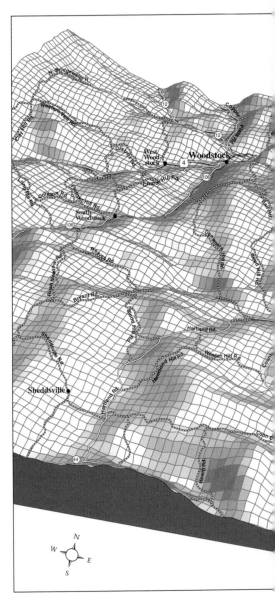

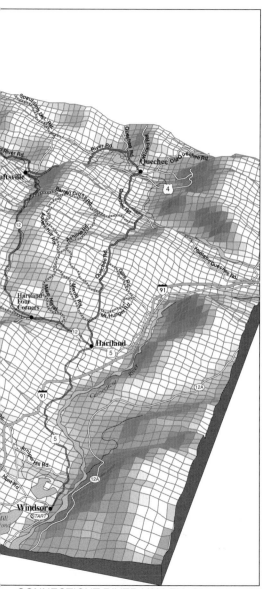

Spaulding Den Rd.

River Rd.

r River Rd.

Quechee Rd.

Old Quechee Rd.

Quechee

Old Quechee Rd.

aftsville

4

12

Barron Circle Rd.

Quechee Rd.

Cloudland Rd.

Shillington

Hartford/Quechee Rd.

Densmore Rd.

Mace Hill Rd.

Quechee Rd.

Clark Rd.

Hartland
Four
Corners

Mt. Hunger Rd.

91

Merrill Rd.

12

Hartland

5

12A

91

Connecticut River

5

12A

Rd.

Juniper Hill Rd.

Hunt Rd.

Windsor

START

Mill
ond

WINDSOR TO WOODSTOCK

Short Route (17.0 miles)

0	Start in downtown Windsor; head north on Rt. 5.
0.7	Constitution House on left; birthplace of Vermont.
1.2	Intersection with Juniper Hill Rd.
3.9	Cross over I-91.
5.0	**Turn left on Rt. 12.**
12.8	**Turn left on Rt. 4;** caution - watch for traffic on Rt. 4.
13.4	**Turn right on ramp to Taftsville Covered Bridge.**
13.5	**Turn left just after bridge on Old River Rd.;** becomes dirt road.
14.9	Riverdell Farm on right.
15.6	Begin pavement.
16.4	Entrance to Billings Farm Museum on left; **turn left at "Y" on Rt. 12.**
16.6	**Turn left; cross bridge over river.**
16.8	**Turn right on Main St. (Rt. 4).**
17.0	End at the town green in Woodstock.

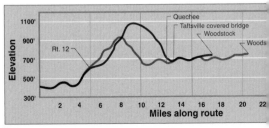

Long Route (20.2 miles)

0	Start in downtown Windsor; head north on Rt. 5.
0.7	Constitution House on left; birthplace of Vermont.
1.2	Intersection with Juniper Hill Rd.
3.9	Cross over Rt. 91.
5.0	**Turn left on Rt. 12; then immediate right onto Quechee Rd.**
6.8	Road becomes dirt.
10.5	Road becomes paved.
12.4	Intersection with Rt. 4; continue straight towards Quechee.
12.5	**Cross the Ottauquechee River and turn left.**
13.3	**Bear left onto River Rd.**
16.7	**Turn right on old River Rd. just before crossing bridge over Ottauquechee River;** becomes dirt road and follows river.
18.1	Riverdell Farm on right.
18.8	Begin pavement.
19.6	Entrance to Billings Farm Museum on left; **left at 'Y' on Rt. 12.**
19.8	**Turn left;** cross bridge over river.
20.0	**Turn right on Main St. (Rt. 4).**
20.2	End at the town green in Woodstock.

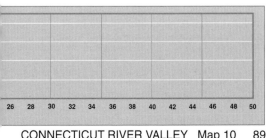

(continued from page 65)

farms and bisected by rushing rivers and streams. Chester and Grafton are both attractive New England villages with interesting architecture and outstanding shops and country inns.

On the third day you head east to the Connecticut River and the wide valley it has carved as it makes its way south to the ocean. The ride north takes on the river's easy-going pace as you pass through the productive farmlands of the valley. Traffic is usually light because cars are diverted to the nearby interstate highway, but the towns of Bellows Falls and Windsor bustle with activity. Bellows Falls, in particular, has an appealing old-time industrial river town feeling about it that makes it seem larger than it really is.

Day four takes you out of the Connecticut River valley to connect with the Ottauquechee River and your return to Woodstock. The long route goes through Quechee, a rebuilt wool mill town that has been developed into a 'second-home' mecca for city dwellers to the south. There are restaurants, shops, and open space along the river. You'll need to use extra caution along the short section of Rt. 4 between Rt. 12 and Taftsville as this road funnels traffic into Woodstock from the interstate freeway and is heavily used.

If you have an extra day to spend cycling in the Woodstock area, head north on Rt. 12. The road works its way up a very pretty valley before climbing a hill and dropping into Barnard. Silver Lake State Park, just outside the hamlet, is a great place for a picnic and swim. You can continue north from the park, on North Rd., over rolling terrain to Bethel, and return to Barnard on Rt. 107 and Rt. 12. There is a short unpaved section of North Rd. about halfway to Bethel.

Heart Of Vermont

This four day route explores the heart of Vermont's hilly interior. The Winooski and Mad River valleys offer a gentle platform for most of the riding, while several side roads venture into the more challenging terrain up from the valley floor.

Stowe is a four-season resort area, as well known for its summer activities as for its winter skiing. Besides being a good launching point for this trip, it lies at the center of many miles of good day cycling (see Stowe Area, page 117). Montpelier is the smallest, and arguably the prettiest, of state capitals. Its small size and many amenities make it a good destination for *(continued on page 116)*

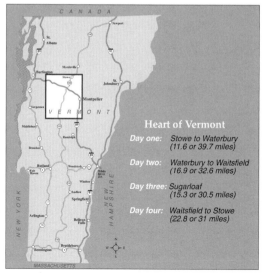

Heart of Vermont

Day one: Stowe to Waterbury
            (11.6 or 39.7 miles)

Day two: Waterbury to Waitsfield
            (16.9 or 32.6 miles)

Day three: Sugarloaf
            (15.3 or 30.5 miles)

Day four: Waitsfield to Stowe
            (22.8 or 31 miles)

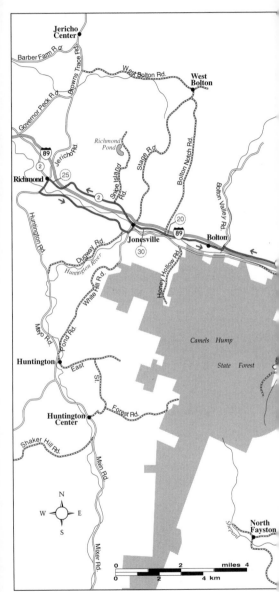

Jericho
Center

Barber Fam R a.

West Bolton Rd.

West
Bolton

Governor Peck Rd.

Browns Trace Rd.

Richmond
Pond

State Rd.

Bolton Notch Rd.

89
2

Jericho Rd.

Snipe Island Rd.

Bolton Valley Rd.

Richmond

25

2

20
89

Jonesville

Bolton

30

Huntington Rd.

Dugway Rd.

Honey Hollow Rd.

Huntington River

White Hill Rd.

Mayo Rd.

Pond Rd.

Huntington

East
St.

Forest Rd.

Camels Hump

Huntington
Center

State Forest

Shaker Hill Rd.

Main Rd.

N
W   E
S

North
Fayston

Shepard

Mixer Rd.

0   2   miles 4
0   2
4 km

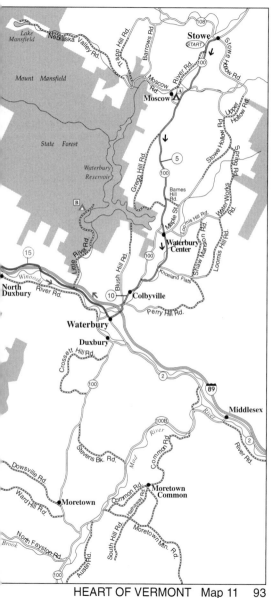

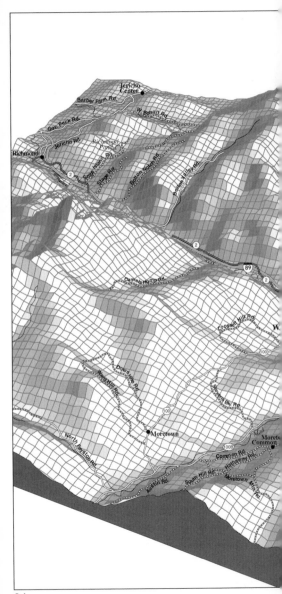

94

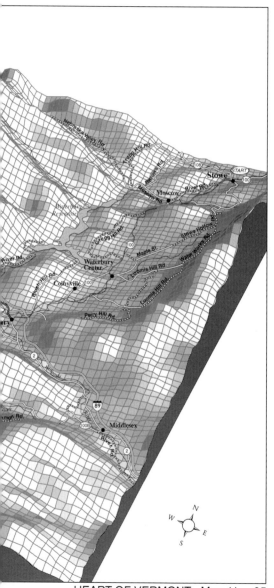

START

Stowe

Moscow

Nebraska Valley Rd.

Trapp Hill Rd.

Randolph Rd.

Moscow Rd.

River Rd.

Gregg Hill Rd.

Maple St.

Stowe Hollow Rd.

Water Works Rd.

Waterbury Center

Loomis Hill Rd.

Colbyville

Branch Hill Rd.

Perry Hill Rd.

River Rd.

Winooski River

Middlesex

River Rd.

N
W · E
S

STOWE TO WATERBURY

Short Route (11.6 miles)

0   Start in downtown Stowe; head south on
         Rt. 100.
2.6   Intersection with Moscow Rd.
**6.9   Turn left at bottom of quick downhill
         where signs point to Waterbury Center,
         Loomis Hill, Barnshill.**
7.2   Turn right on Guptil Rd.; entering
         Waterbury Center.
         *Note: For a dip in Waterbury Reservoir,
         head due west toward Rt. 100. Turn right
         on Rt. 100. Turn right on Rt. 100, then
         immediate left to the reservoir. Cost $1.50.*
9.2   Turn left on Rt. 100.
9.6   Ben and Jerry's Ice Cream Factory on the
         right; tours available.
10.6   Turn left just before I-89 interchange.
11.1   Cross under I-89.
11.6   End at the intersection with South Main
         St. (Rt. 2) in Waterbury.

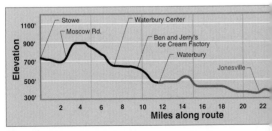

Long Route (39.7miles)

0   Start in downtown Stowe; follow short route
directions to Waterbury Center.

**11.6 Turn right on South Main St. (Rt. 2) in
Waterbury.**

14.1 Great view of Camel's Hump to the left.

21.7 Jonesville.

25.3 Turn left at traffic light in Richmond;

25.7 Cross over an iron bridge.

25.9 Round Church on the left; nice spot
for a rest.

26.0 Turn left after the Church.

26.4 Cemetery on the right.

29.1 Turn left at the 'Y'.
*Note: For a swim in Huntington Gorge
(add 3 miles) turn right at the 'Y' up the
dirt road with "Cars parked in travelled
section of roadway will be towed" sign.
Continue past Paramount Morgan Horse
Farm. Look for cliffs and a deep chasm on
your left. Use the pull-out above the gorge
where the stream is only 10 feet below the
road- it's the most accessible and best
swimming hole!*

29.3 Road bends left at a red barn.

29.5 Cross an iron bridge over the Winooski River.

29.6 Turn right on Rt. 2.

39.7 End at the traffic light in Waterbury.

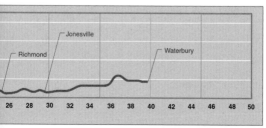

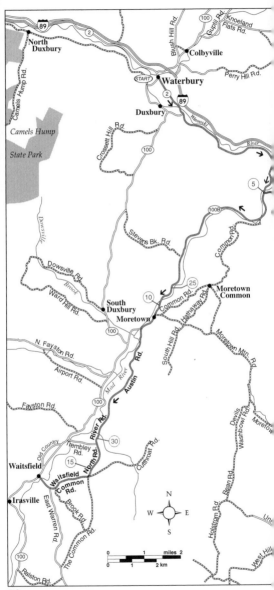

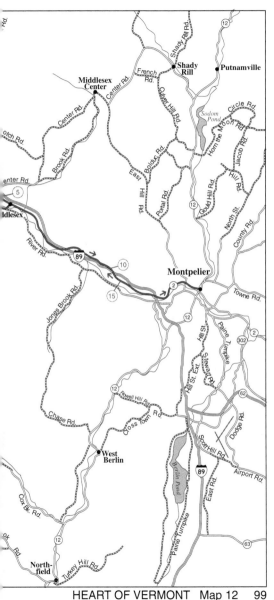

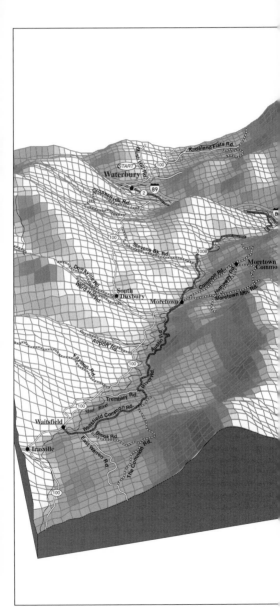

START
Waterbury
Knealand Flats Rd.
100
2
89
Crossett Hill Rd.
100
Stevens Bk. Rd.
100B
Moretown
Common Rd.
Hadley Rd.
Moretown
Common
Dowsville Rd.
Herd Hill Rd.
South
Duxbury
Moretown
Moretown Mtn. Rd.
Airport Rd.
Ferggson Rd.
100
River Rd.
Austin Rd.
Trembley Rd.
Mad River
100
Moldsfield Common Rd.
Waitsfield
Brook Rd.
East Warren Rd.
Trasville
The Common Rd.
100

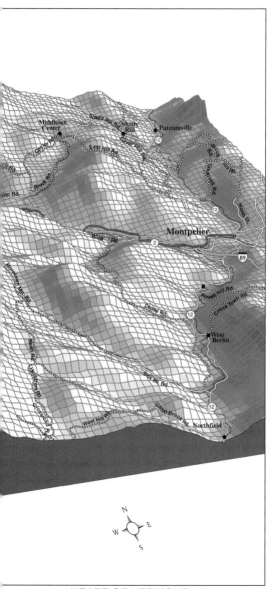

Middlesex
Center

Shady Rill Rd.

Shady
Rill

Putnamsville

12

Center Rd.

East Hill Rd.

River Hill Rd.

Horn of the Moon Rd.

Chase Hill Rd.

Brook Rd.

Sister Rd.

12

North St.

Rice Rd.

Montpelier

2

89

Montpelier Wtn. Rd.

Chase Rd.

Dodge Hill Rd.

Cross Town Rd.

12

West
Berlin

Bear Rd.

Lightning Rd.

Cox Bk. Rd.

Crossroad Rd.

West Hill Rd.

Union Brook Rd.

Northfield

12

N
W   E
S

WATERBURY TO WAITSFIELD

Short Route (16.9 miles)

0   Start in the center of Waterbury at the traffic light; head east on Rt. 2.
1.0   Intersection with Rt. 100.
4.1   **Turn right on dirt road (unsigned) just before the green steel bridge.**
4.9   **Bear left at the fork and cross over bridge;**
5.0   **Turn right on Rt. 100B.**
7.0   Kenneth Ward Recreation Area on left; good spot for a picnic and a swim!
10.3   Moretown.
10.7   **Turn left onto dirt road .3 miles after two churches on left and just after road curves to the right;** begin uphill.
     Note: There is a 3.7 section of dirt road along this route. To stay on pavement, continue south on Rt. 100 to Waitsfield.
12.0   Carpenter Farm Inn on the left.
13.0   Continue straight past a road on the right.
14.7   Begin pavement; continue straight past White Pine Dr. on the right.
15.3   **Turn right at cemetery to stay on pavement.**
16.5   **Turn right at 'T' on East Warren Rd.**
16.8   '1833' covered bridge; great swimming hole under the bridge.
16.9   End in Waitsfield at the intersection with Rt. 100.

Long Route (continued)
31.0   **Turn right at cemetery to stay on pavement.**
32.2   **Turn right at 'T' on East Warren Rd.**
32.5   '1833' covered bridge.
32.6   End in Waitsfield at the intersection with Rt. 100.

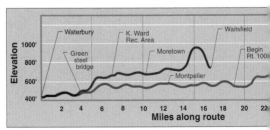

Long Route (32.6 miles)

0	Start in the center of Waterbury at the traffic light; head east on Rt. 2.
1.0	Intersection with Rt. 100.
4.1	Intersection with dirt road cut-off to Rt. 100B (short route); continue straight over the green steel bridge.
5.4	Intersection with Rt. 100B.
7.5	Cross over I-89.
10.1	Cross under I-89.
11.4	Cross under I-89.
11.6	Green Mountain Cemetery on the left.
12.4	Continue straight on State St. at the traffic light; there are good spots to eat in Montpelier; **turn around point;** retrace route west on Rt. 2.
19.4	**Turn left on Rt. 100B.**
20.7	Intersection with dirt road cut-off from Rt.2 (short route); continue south on Rt. 100B.
21.5	Bridge over Mad River.
22.7	Kenneth Ward Recreation Area on left; good spot for a picnic and a swim!
26.0	Moretown.
26.4	**Turn left onto dirt road .3 miles after two churches on left and just after road curves to right;** begin uphill climb. *Note: There is a 3.7 mile section of dirt road along this route. To stay on pavement, continue south on Rt. 100 to Waitsfield.*
27.7	Carpenter Farm Inn on the left.
28.7	Continue straight past a road on the right.
29.8	Covered bridge.
30.1	Begin pavement; continue straight past a road on the right; begin uphill climb.
30.4	Continue straight past White Pine Dr. on the right.

(continued on left)

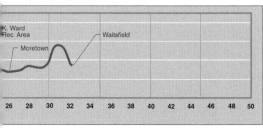

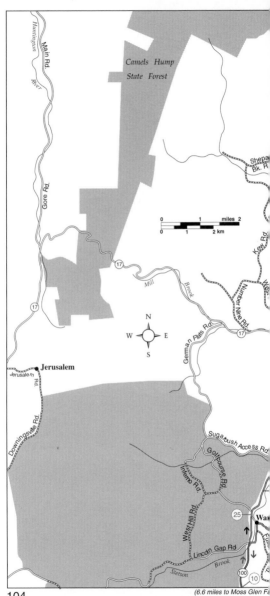

Camels Hump
State Forest

Huntington River

Main Rd.

Gore Rd.

Shepa_
Bk. R.

0   1   miles 2
0   1   2 km

17

Key Rd.

Mill   Brook

Wes_

Number Nine Rd.

17

N
W   E
S

German Flats Rd.

Jerusalem

Jerusalem m_

Downingsvile Rd.

Sugarbush Access Rd

Golbourse Rd.

Inferno Rd.

West Hill Rd.

25   **Wa**_

Flu_

Lincoln Gap Rd

Brook

Stetson

100   10

104

(6.6 miles to Moss Glen Fa_

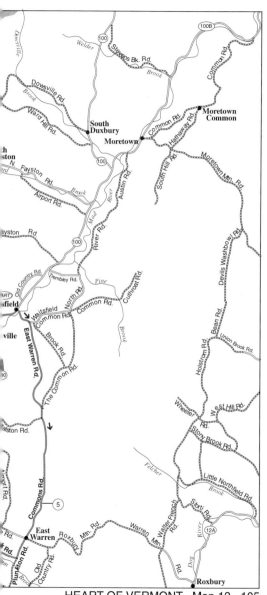

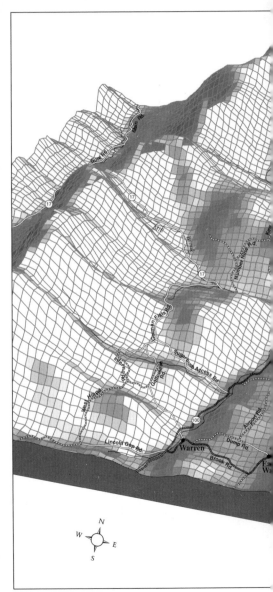

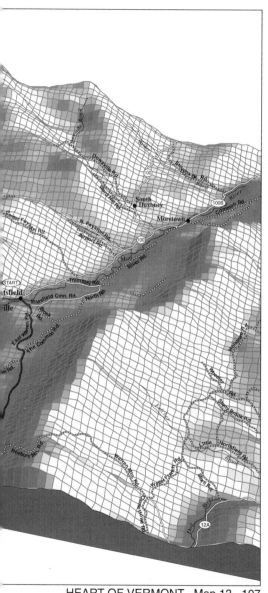

START
tsfield
ille

Dowsville Road
Dowsville Rd.
Kneel Hill Rd.
100
South
Duxbury
100B
Common Rd.
River
Moretown
Stevens Br. Rd.
Mad
N. Fayston Rd.
Airport Rd.
100
Mud
River Rd.
Tremblay Rd.
Fenton Farm Rd.
Waitsfield Cmn. Rd.
North Rd.
Brook
Rd.
East Warren Rd.
The Common Rd.
Holman Rd.
Wheeler Rd.
Shady Brook Rd.
Little
Northfield Rd.
Little
River
Roxbury Mtn. Rd.
Warren Alps Rd.
Mill Brook Rd.
East
Roxbury
Cox Brook Rd.
Dugway Rd.
Sherr Rd.
12A

WARREN

Short Route (15.3 miles)

0   Start at the intersection of Rt. 100 and East
         Warren Rd. in Waitsfield; head southeast on
         E. Warren Rd.
0.1   Cross the '1833' covered bridge.
0.4   Bear right to stay on East Warren Rd.
**2.6   Bear right to continue on paved E.
         Warren Rd.**
5.5   Schafer Farm on right.
6.0   East Warren; continue straight through
         four-way intersection (Dump Rd.).
         Note: For 2 mile detour to the airport:
         Turn right on Dump Rd.; go .5 mile then
         right on Airport Rd.; .5 mile to Warren
         Airport. Glider rides offered!
6.6   Bear right; becomes Brook Rd.
8.3   Continue straight on Brook Rd.
8.4   Turn left at the yield sign in Warren; good
         food and toy store on right and a nice lunch
         spot just up the road.
**8.7   Turn right to cross covered bridge; then
         left towards Rt. 100.**
8.8   Turn right on Rt. 100.
10.5   Continue straight on Rt. 100 at intersection
         with road to Sugarbush.
11.0   Bridge over Mad River.
14.2   Irasville.
15.3   End at East Warren Rd. in Waitsfield.

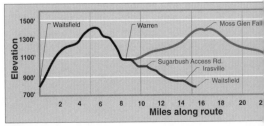

MOSS GLEN FALLS

Long Route (30.5 miles)

Start at the intersection of Rt. 100 and E. Warren Rd. in Waitsfield; follow the short route directions to mile 8.8 in Warren.

8.8 **Turn left on Rt. 100 heading south.**

6.4 Moss Glen Falls on the right; **turn around point.**

3.7 Intersection with road into Warren; continue straight on Rt. 100.

9.4 Irasville.

0.5 End at E. Warren Rd. in Waitsfield.

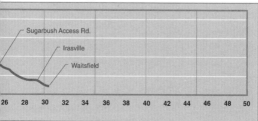

Sugarbush Access Rd.

Irasville

Waitsfield

26 28 30 32 34 36 38 40 42 44 46 48 50

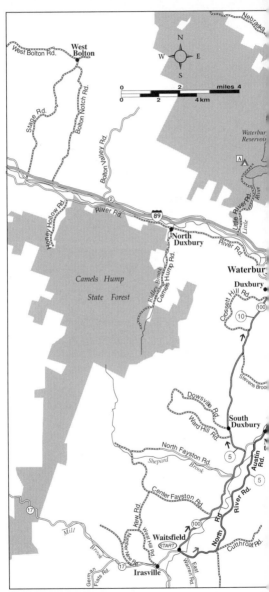

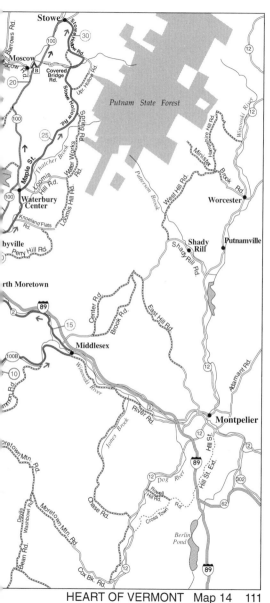

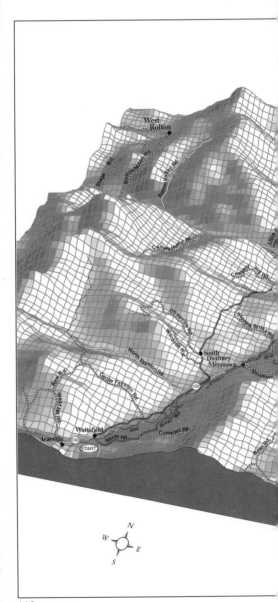

West Bolton

Stage Rd.

Bolton Valley Rd.

Bolton Valley Rd.

Camel Hump Rd.

Little

Crossett Hill Rd.

Duxbury Rd.

Winsfield Rd.

North Fayston Rd.

South Duxbury
Moretown

Stevens Brook Rd.

River

Moretown

Kew Rd.

Center Fayston Rd.

100

Irasville

Waitsfield

100

START

North Rd.

Mill

River Rd.

Cuthroat Rd.

Brim Rd.

N
W · E
S

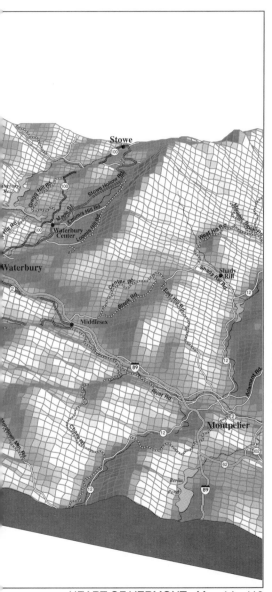

WAITSFIELD TO STOWE

Short Route (22.8 miles)

0   Start in Waitsfield at the intersection of Rt. 100 and East Warren Rd.; head north on Rt. 100.
4.4   Turn left to stay on Rt. 100 where Rt. 100B continues straight.
11.6   Turn left on Rt. 2.
11.8   Cross Winooski River.
11.9   Bear left at the fork; entering Waterbury.
12.0   Continue straight through first set of lights.
12.3   Turn right at second set of lights (gas station and bank).
12.8   Cross under I-89.
13.1   Turn right on Rt. 100 North.
13.5   Thatcher Brook Inn on right.
13.8   Ben & Jerry's Ice Cream Factory; tours and the best ice cream around; good lunch spot.
15.9   Cold Hollow Cider Mill on right.
20.2   Intersection with Moscow Rd.
22.8   End in downtown Stowe.

Long Route (continued)

26.4   Bear left to stay on Stowe Hollow Rd.; becomes Covered Bridge Rd.
26.9   Begin paved road.
27.2   Begin dirt road.
28.3   Begin paved road.
28.4   Turn right to stay on Stowe Hollow Rd. where Gold Brook Rd. goes left.
29.0   Turn left to stay on Stowe Hollow Rd. where Upper Hollow Rd. goes right.
30.9   Turn left on Rt. 100 in Stowe.
31.0   End at Rt. 108 in downtown Stowe.

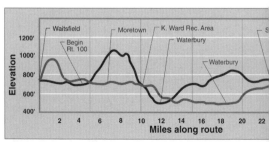

Long Route (31.0 miles)

0   Start in Waitsfield at the intersection of Rt. 100 and East Warren Rd.; head southeast on East Warren Rd.

0.4   Turn left on Waitsfield Common Rd. (1st paved road after bridge).
1.6   Cemetery on left.
1.7   Continue straight on paved road at intersection.
2.3   White Pine Dr. on left.
2.6   Continue straight past paved road on left.
2.8   Begin dirt road.
2.9   Covered bridge.
4.0   Continue straight past dirt road on left.
6.3   Turn right on Rt. 100B.
6.8   Moretown.
7.3   Iron bridge over Mad River.
10.1   Kenneth Ward Recreataion Area on right; good spot for a picnic and a swim!
13.3   Turn left on Rt. 2.
17.8   Intersection with Rt. 100.
18.1   Bear left at the fork; entering Waterbury.
18.2   Continue straight through first set of lights.
18.5   Turn right at second set of lights (gas station and bank).
19.0   Cross under I-89.
19.3   Turn right on Rt. 100 North.
19.7   Thatcher Brook Inn on right.
20.7   Turn right on Guptil Rd. toward Waterbury Center.
21.4   Cross bridge and stay left.
22.7   Waterbury Center; **turn right on Maple St.;** becomes Stowe Hollow Rd.
23.9   Intersection with Barnes Hill Rd.
25.0   Begin dirt road.
26.4   Bear left to stay on Stowe Hollow Rd.; becomes Covered Bridge Rd.

(continued on left)

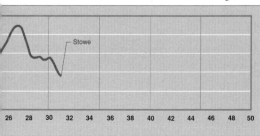

HEART OF VERMONT   Map 14   115

(continued from page 91)

cyclists. The closeness of the interstate highway parallel to Rt. 2 draws much of the traffic from that road, making access to the city by bike quite comfortable. Further south, ski resorts have heavily influenced the character of the area around Waitsfield and Warren, – creating a wide variety of accommodations and eating places. Interspersed among these, and other 'large' towns, are many smaller villages, both quaint and ordinary.

Expect to find a variety of riding conditions in these four days. Routes 100, 100B, and 2 are generally flatter, wider, and more heavily trafficked than the other roads that make up the profiled routes. The secondary, smaller roads include short sections of dirt and often wander up into the hills. They also offer some of the best views, opportunities for a special sight or swim, and pass through some of the more picturesque small villages in the region.

Route 100 is considered one of the prettiest roads in Vermont and draws many touring motorists. Traffic is especially heavy in the fall foliage season (mid-September to early October), though extra caution should be exercised at all times.

Stowe
Area

The Stowe area has long been a destination for winter sports enthusiasts. Its four-season recreation reputation has been almost as strong, and cycling has been an essential part of that reputation. Many people mix their cycling with other activities that are found in abundance in the area. Besides resort-oriented recreation like tennis and golf, there is easy access to hiking, canoeing, fishing, camping, horseback riding, and stream and lake swimming.

Mount Mansfield, Vermont's highest mountain (4,393'), lies at the heart of a ridge of mountains to the west of Stowe. *(continued on page 126)*

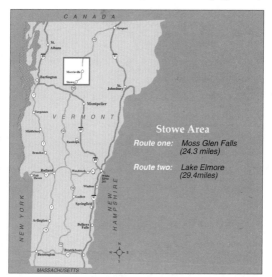

Stowe Area

Route one: Moss Glen Falls (24.3 miles)

Route two: Lake Elmore (29.4 miles)

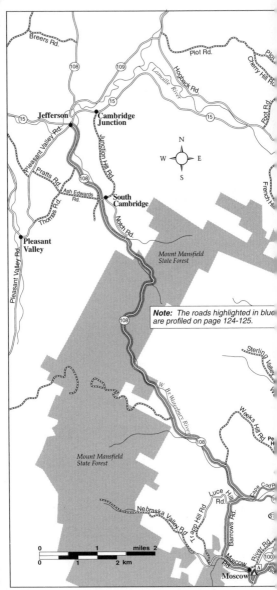

Breers Rd.

Plot Rd.

Cherry Hill Rd

108

109

Hogback Rd.

Lamoille River

Foot Rd.

15

Jefferson

Cambridge Junction

15

Pleasant Valley Rd.

N
W   E
S

Pratts Rd.

108

Junction Hill Rd.

Ash Edwards Rd.

South Cambridge

Thomas Rd.

Notch Rd.

French H

Pleasant Valley

Mount Mansfield State Forest

Pleasant Valley Rd.

108

Note: The roads highlighted in blue are profiled on page 124-125.

Sterling Valley

W

W. Br. Waterbury River

108

Weeks Hill Rd

Pe
H

Mount Mansfield State Forest

Luce Hill Rd

Cape Cod R

Trapp Hill Rd

Barrows Rd.

Nebraska Valley Rd.

0   1   miles 2
0   1   2 km

Moscow Rd.

River Rd.

100

A1

Moscow

118

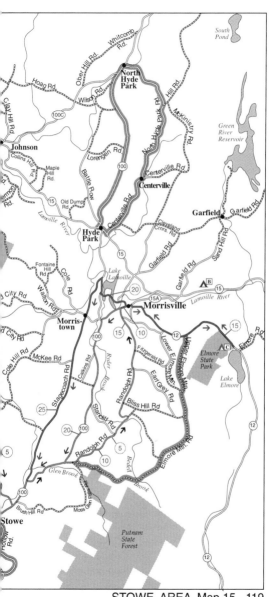

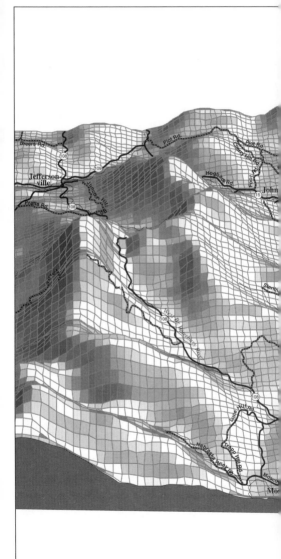

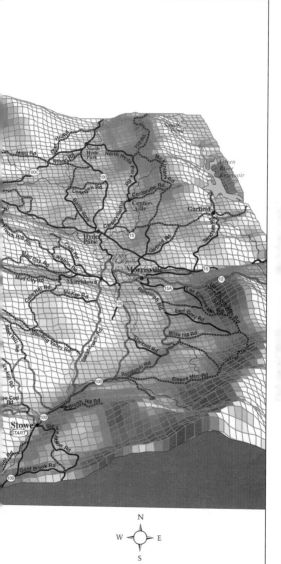

W E

N

S

ANOTHER MOSS GLEN FALLS

24.3 miles

0	Start in Stowe at the intersection of Rt. 100 and Rt. 108; head west on Rt. 108.
1.6	**Turn right on Cape Cod Rd.**
2.1	Keep to the right at the fork, passing the Stowe Country Club.
2.8	**Turn left at the stop sign.**
3.2	Bridge over brook.
3.8	**Bear right at the fork on Percy Hill Rd.**
4.4	**Turn right at stop sign on West Hill Rd.**
4.7	Keep to the right at the fork.
6.3	Bridge over creek.
6.6	**Turn left on Rt. 100 North.**
8.9	**Turn right on Randolph Rd.**
	Note: To visit Moss Glen Falls, turn right at the sign for the School of Art and go .5 miles. Turn left into an unpaved pull-over area just before a small bridge. Pull your bike into the path a little and hike to the falls. It's about a 1/4 mile walk - there are many paths.
9.3	Keep left at intersection of Elmore Mtn. Rd.
15.6	**Turn left on Rt. 100 S.**
21.2	Intersection with Randolph Rd.
23.4	Intersection with West Hill Rd.
24.3	End in Stowe at intersection of Rt. 100 and Rt. 108.

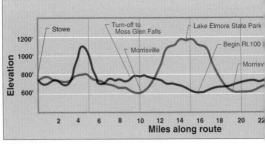

LAKE ELMORE

29.4 miles

0   Start in Stowe at the intersection of Rt. 100 and Rt. 108; head north on Rt. 100.

0.8   Intersection with West Hill Rd.

1.7   Intersection with Stagecoach Rd.

3.0   Bear right on Randolph Rd.

3.4   Keep left at intersection with Elmore Mtn. Rd.

9.8   Turn right on Rt. 100 North.

10.1   Morrisville; continue straight through blinking light.

10.3   Bear right, staying on Rt. 12.

12.2   Intersection with Elmore Mtn. Rd.

14.5   Turn right into Lake Elmore State Park.
$1.50 entry. Swimming, rest rooms, and snack area. **Turn around point.**

19.0   Turn right, then left in Morrisville to cross the Lamoille River on Bridge St.

20.1   Turn right on Cadys Falls Rd.

20.6   Turn left on Stagecoach Rd.

27.6   Join Rt. 100 South.

28.5   Intersection with West Hill Rd.

29.4   End in Stowe at intersection of Rt. 100 & Rt. 108.

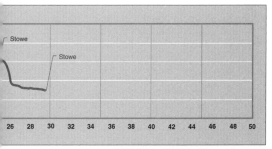

MOSCOW LOOP

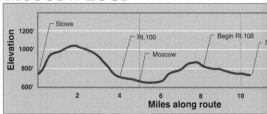

ELMORE MOUNTAIN ROAD

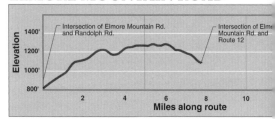

ROUTE 108

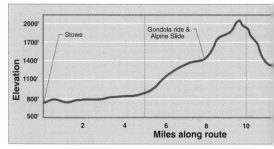

HYDE PARK LOOP

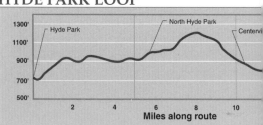

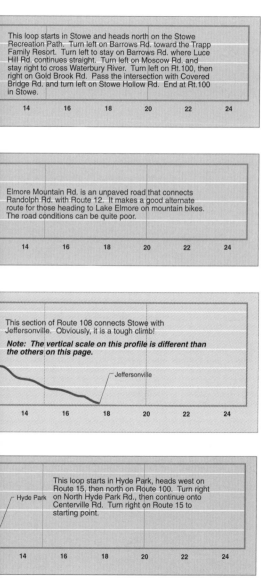

This loop starts in Stowe and heads north on the Stowe Recreation Path. Turn left on Barrows Rd. toward the Trapp Family Resort. Turn left to stay on Barrows Rd. where Luce Hill Rd. continues straight. Turn left on Moscow Rd. and stay right to cross Waterbury River. Turn left on Rt.100, then right on Gold Brook Rd. Pass the intersection with Covered Bridge Rd. and turn left on Stowe Hollow Rd. End at Rt.100 in Stowe.

14   16   18   20   22   24

Elmore Mountain Rd. is an unpaved road that connects Randolph Rd. with Route 12. It makes a good alternate route for those heading to Lake Elmore on mountain bikes. The road conditions can be quite poor.

14   16   18   20   22   24

This section of Route 108 connects Stowe with Jeffersonville. Obviously, it is a tough climb!

Note: The vertical scale on this profile is different than the others on this page.

Jeffersonville

14   16   18   20   22   24

Hyde Park

This loop starts in Hyde Park, heads west on Route 15, then north on Route 100. Turn right on North Hyde Park Rd., then continue onto Centerville Rd. Turn right on Route 15 to starting point.

14   16   18   20   22   24

(continued from page 117)

Between Interstate 89 to the south and Hwy. 15 to the north, only Rt. 108 crosses this ridge. There are many hiking trails in Mt. Mansfield State Forest, and a popular gondola ride will take you close to the summit. East of Stowe is another mountain ridge, straddled by the Putnam State Forest, which also forms a barrier to bikes and vehicles. Rt. 100 runs the length of the valley between the two ridges, and there are many roads, mostly unpaved, that penetrate their lower slopes. Stowe is the center of activity in the valley, offering many choices for accommodations and eating.

The Stowe Recreation Path is a paved biking and walking trail that parallels Rt. 108 through its most densely developed section. It provides a good link from the lodging in that area to 'downtown' Stowe, and to the routes profiled here. We have described two routes in detail on the following pages, and have provided profiles for several more roads on pages 124 and 125. While the mountains limit the number of east-west routes, there are several areas to bike north and south of town. Tossing your bike in the car and taking a short drive north opens up even more good road riding.

Richard Hubbard and Rose Marie Matulionis, proprietors of the historic 1860 House Bed and Breakfast in Stowe, have hosted visiting cyclists for years and enjoy helping plan a day's ride. They'll provide a safe place to store a bike and even space for repair work. Stowe also has several shops that rent and service bikes, and that are usually good sources of information and suggestions.

Mountain biking in the hills and valleys around Stowe is becoming increasingly popular. There is a good network of unpaved roads, and most are well suited to fat-tire exploration. The terrain is steep in places, and the road surfaces vary in quality. Again, get some local suggestions for rides to suit your skill and endurance level. Hiking trails, private roads, and logging roads are usually closed to mountain bikes.

Cape Islands

You can't do much better than Martha's Vineyard and Nantucket for a cycling retreat. They are big enough to let you stretch your limits for a day's ride, but small enough to provide many destinations for a short and easy jaunt. You'll find many miles of well-maintained country roads, plenty of great views, and good access to the beach.

On Martha's Vineyard there are a few roads that carry most of the traffic around the island, and you can often find good alternate routes if these are too busy. The eastern half of the island is more heavily settled, and offers the kinds of amenities associated with a well-developed tourist trade. Vineyard Haven, Oak Bluffs, and Edgartown are the island's *(continued on page 140)*

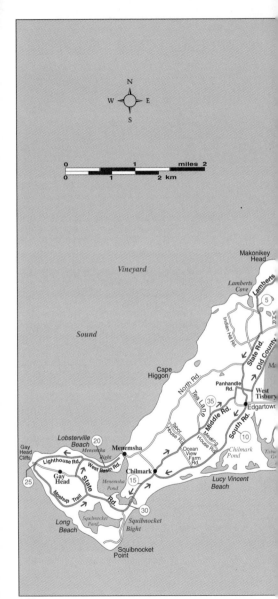

N
W E
S

0   1   miles 2
0   1   2 km

Vineyard

Sound

Makonikey
Head

*Lamberts
Cove*

Lamberts

(5)

V
H
R

Indian Hill Rd.

Cape
Higgon

North Rd.

State Rd.

Old County

Ma

Panhandle
Rd.

Tea Lane

West
Tisbury

(35)

Middle Rd.

Edgartown

Tabor
House Rd.

Meeting
House Rd.

South Rd.

(10)

Lobsterville
Beach
(20)

*Menemsha
Bight*

Menemsha

West Basin Rd.

Ocean View
Farm Rd.

*Chilmark
Pond*

Tisbu
Gr

Gay
Head
Cliffs

Lighthouse Rd.

Chilmark

(15)

Lucy Vincent
Beach

(25)

Gay
Head

State

Rd.

*Menemsha
Pond*

Mohup Trail

(30)

*Long
Beach*

*Squibnocket
Pond*

*Squibnocket
Bight*

Squibnocket
Point

128

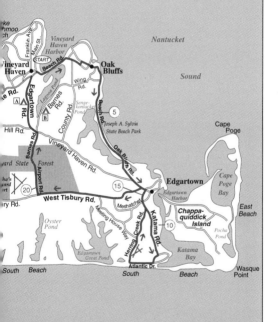

Martha's Vineyard

ke
hmoo
ch

Franklin Ave.

Main St.

Vineyard
Haven
Harbor

START

Beach Rd.

Oak Bluffs

Nantucket

Vineyard
Haven

e Rd.

A

Edgartown Rd.

B

Barnes Rd.

Lagoon Pond

Wing Rd.

Senge-
komlacker
Pond

County Rd.

Beach Rd.

5

Joseph A. Sylvia State Beach Park

Sound

Cape
Poge

Hill Rd.

Barnes Rd.

Vineyard Haven Rd.

Oak Bluffs Rd.

Edgartown

Edgartown Harbor

*Cape
Poge
Bay*

yard State

Forest

Airport Rd.

a's
yard
ort

20

West Tisbury Rd.

15

Meshatchet

Meeting House Way

Katama Rd.

*Chappa-
quiddick
Island*

*East
Beach*

ury Rd.

*Oyster
Pond*

Herring Creek Rd.

10

*Edgartown
Great Pond*

*Katama
Bay*

*Pocha
Pond*

South   Beach

Atlantic Dr.

South

Beach

*Wasque
Point*

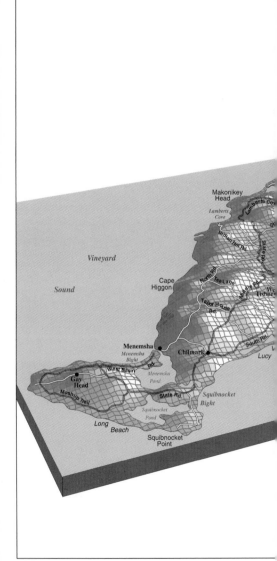

Makonikey
Head

*Lamberts
Cove*

Vineyard

Sound

Cape
Higgon

North Rd.

Tabor House
Rd.

Menemsha

*Menemsha
Bight*

West Basin

Chillmark

South Rd.

Lucy

*Menemsha
Pond*

**Gay
Head**

Moshup Trail

State Rd.

*Squibnocket
Bight*

*Squibnocket
Pond*

*Long
Beach*

Squibnocket
Point

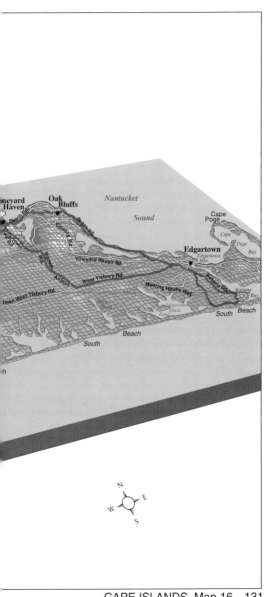

neyard
Haven

Oak
Bluffs

Nantucket

Cape
Poge

Sound

Beach Rd.

County Rd.

Beach Rd.

Cape
Poge
Bay

Edgartown

Edgartown
Rd.

Vineyard Haven Rd.

Airport

Edgartown
Hbr.

town West Tisbury Rd.

West Tisbury Rd.

Meeting House Way

Katama Rd.

Katama
Bay

Orchard
Beach

Edgartown
Great
Pond

South Beach

Beach

South Beach

h

N
W ✦ E
S

MARTHA'S VINEYARD

Gay Head (43.3 miles)

0	Start at the ferry landing in Vineyard Haven; **turn left after coming off the ferry dock.**
0.1	**Turn right at first intersection towards Gay Head.**
0.2	**Bear left onto South Main St.;** becomes State Rd.
1.7	**Turn right on Lamberts Cove Rd.**
5.1	Seth's Pond on left; small swimming beach.
5.9	**Turn right on State Rd.**
7.3	Intersection with North Rd.
8.2	Intersection with Panhandle Rd.
8.8	**Bear right following signs to Chilmark and Gay Head.**
8.9	West Tisbury; Alley General Store and Post Office.
13.0	Allen Farm Sheep and Wool Co. on right (great sweaters and blankets).
14.1	Beetleburg Corner; **turn left at fork towards Gay Head.**
14.3	Chilmark. *Note: for 25.5 mile loop - turn right on Middle Rd. and pick up directions at 31.9 miles.*
18.3	**Turn right on Lobsterville Rd. toward Lobsterville Beach.**
19.2	Intersection with Lighthouse Rd.
19.9	**Turn left towards beach.**
20.9	**Turn around point** (dead end).
22.6	**Turn right on Lighthouse Rd.**
24.6	**Turn right at 'T';** lighthouse on right.
24.7	Gay Head Cliffs; viewpoint and restaurant; toilets.
25.0	**Turn right on Moshup's Trail.**
28.3	**Turn right at 'T' on South Rd.**
31.7	Chilmark.
31.9	Bettlebung Corner; continue straight at 'Y' onto Middle Rd.
36.4	**Turn left at 'T' on Panhandle Rd.**

(continued on right)

Note: This vertical scale is more exaggerated than the vertical scale on the Vermont and Maine profiles.

Edgartown (24.5 miles)

	Start at the ferry landing in Vineyard Haven; **turn left after coming off the ferry dock.**
.1	**Turn left on Beach Rd. toward Oak Bluffs.**
.5	**Turn left towards Oak Bluffs.**
.3	Lobster Hatchery on right.
.0	Oak Bluffs.
.1	**Turn right at ocean.**
.6	Bike path on right.
.4	**Turn right on Peases Point Rd. towards Katama Rd.**; becomes Katama Rd. *Note: Follow bike path and signs to get to Edgartown and the ferry to Chappaquiddick Island.*
.2	Intersection with Herring Creek Rd.
1.1	**Turn right to stay on main road.**
1.6	**Turn right to ride west along beach front.**
2.5	**Turn right on Herring Creek Rd.**
4.6	**Bear left on Katama Rd.**
5.4	**Turn left on Main St./Vineyard Haven Rd.**
5.5	**Turn left on West Tisbury Rd. at Depot Corner gas station.**
7.9	Bike path begins.
9.5	**Turn right on Barnes Rd. toward Vineyard Haven.**
1.8	**Turn left on Edgartown Vineyard Haven Rd.**
4.0	**Turn right on State Rd.**
4.5	End at the ferry landing.

***ay Head** (continued)*

7.2	Continue straight across State Rd.
7.6	**Turn left on Old County Rd.**
0.1	**Turn right on State Rd.**
1.6	Intersection with Lamberts Cove Rd.
3.3	End at the ferry landing.

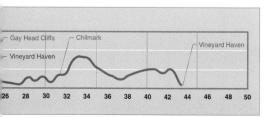

Nantucket Island

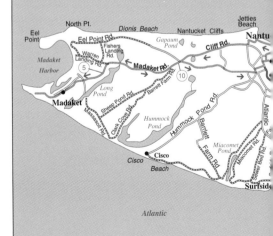

134

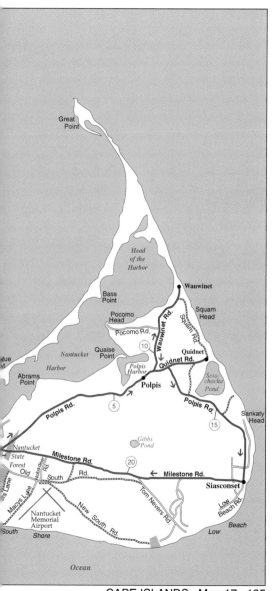

Great
Point

Head
of the
Harbor

Wauwinet

Bass
Point

Squam
Head

Pocomo
Head

Pocomo Rd.

Quidnet

Nantucket

(10)

Quaise
Point

Wauwinet Rd.

Squam Rd.

Quidnet Rd.

Abrams
Point

Harbor

Polpis
Harbor

Polpis

Sesachacha
Pond

Polpis Rd.

Polpis Rd.

(5)

(15)

Sankaty
Head

Nantucket

Gibbs
Pond

State
Forest

Milestone Rd.

(20)

Milestone Rd.

Old

Rd.

Siasconset

Macys Lane

Nantucket
Memorial
Airport

New South Rd.

Tom Nevers Rd.

Low
Beach Rd.

South

Shore

Low

Beach

Ocean

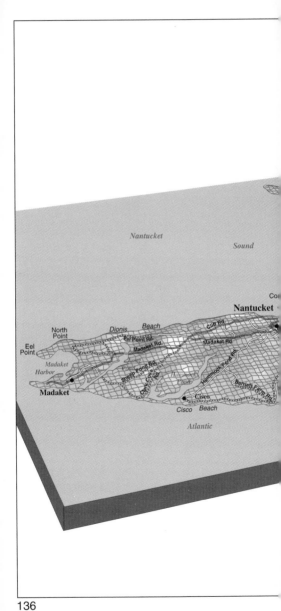

Nantucket

Sound

Coa

Nantucket

North
Point

Dionis   Beach

Cliff Rd.

Eel
Point

Eel Point Rd.

Madaket Rd.

Madaket Rd.

*Madaket
Harbor*

Sheep Pond Rd.

Clear Cove Rd.

*Hummock
Pond*

Hummock Pond Rd.

Barrett Farm Rd.

Madaket

Cisco

Cisco   Beach

Atlantic

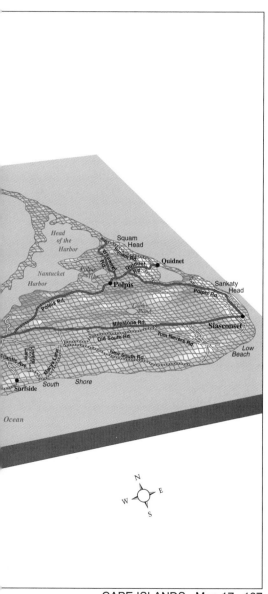

NANTUCKET

Short route (12.4 miles)

0   Start at the Steamboat Wharf in Nantucket;
       turn right on S. Beach.
0.2   Turn right on Easton.
**0.3   Turn left on Hulbert Ave. at the Coast
       Guard Station.**
**0.8   Turn left on Bathing Beach Rd.
       Turn right on N. Beach.
       Turn left on Cobblestone Hill.**
**0.9   Turn left on Grant Ave.
       Turn right on Nantucket Ave.**
1.0   Turn right on Cliff Rd.
2.9   Intersection with Eel Pt. Rd. and Madaket
       Rd.; continue straight onto Madaket Rd.
6.5   Madaket; **turn around point.**
10.1   Intersection with Eel Pt. Rd.; continue on
       Madaket Rd. towards Nantucket.
11.8   Straight at rotary onto Upper Main St.;
       Quaker Cemetary on right.
**12.0   Turn left at rotary (war memorial) onto
       Gardner.**
12.1   Turn right on India.
**12.2   Turn left on Center.
       Turn right on Broad.**
12.4   End at the Steamboat Wharf.

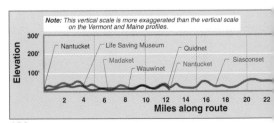

Long route (25.1 miles)

0	Start at the Steamboat Wharf in Nantucket. **Turn left on S. Water St.** **Turn right on Main St.** (cobblestone pavement).
0.2	**Turn left on Orange St.**
1.1	**Turn left at rotary onto Milestone Rd.**
1.4	**Turn left on Polpis Rd.**
3.9	Life Saving Museum on left; good view.
6.0	**Turn left at fork toward Wauwinet (Wauwinet Rd.).**
6.5	Nantucket School of Design and the Arts on right.
8.3	Road ends at Wauwinet House; **turn around point.**
10.6	**Turn left on Polpis Rd.**
11.0	**Turn left at fork towards Quidnet.**
12.1	**Turn left at the intersection to go to the 'pond' and the ocean; turn around point.**
13.2	**Turn left on Polpis Rd. to Siasconset.**
17.0	Siasconset; **turn left at rotary to the beach; leave Siasconset on Milestone Rd.** (there is a bike path along this road).
24.0	**Bear right at rotary onto Orange St.**
24.9	Intersection with Main St.
25.0	**Turn right on Broad St.**
25.1	End at the Steamboat Wharf.

Nantucket

| 26 | 28 | 30 | 32 | 34 | 36 | 38 | 40 | 42 | 44 | 46 | 48 | 50 |

(continued from page 127)

main towns and each has a wide assortment of restaurants and shops. It's pretty easy to design an enjoyable day that combines bike riding, playing in the ocean, and finding a good meal on this side of the island. Besides the small beaches in all three towns, the Joseph Sylvia State Beach between Oak Bluffs and Edgartown, and South Beach at the end of Katama Rd. are both public beaches.

The western half of Martha's Vineyard has a more rural character. Lunch options are limited to picnics or picking up a snack at Gay Head Cliffs. There are food stores in North Tisbury, West Tisbury, Chilmark, and Menemsha. Lobsterville Beach, along West Basin Rd., would make a choice picnic and swimming destination for the day's ride. Other public beaches include the Menemsha Town Beach, Menemsha Pond Beach at the end of West Basin Rd., and Long Beach on the southwestern coast. The multicolored Gay Head Cliffs are one of the island's main attractions, and the public restrooms located nearby make them even more attractive to cyclists.

While there is a passenger ferry between the two islands, Nantucket is accessible to autos only from Hyannis on Cape Cod. See page 16 for ferry information. Some people find Nantucket to be even more quaint and appealing than Martha's Vineyard. It is fairly flat and offers a wealth of natural beauty and historic interest. Quidnet, on the long route, is a wonderful little town – a good place for a stroll. In addition to the main roads followed by the routes in this guide, you'll find plenty of opportunities to explore the back roads of the island, though not many of them are paved.

Maine's
Mid-Coast

At the hub of these routes is the small town of Camden. As both a fishing village and popular yachting center, Camden offers the scenic richness of coastal Maine and the amenities of a first class vacation center. Great accommodations, a variety of restaurants, shops and galleries, and an active harbor scene make it an excellent place to start and end a day's ride.

Rockport, just south of Camden, is a picturesque seaside village. It is a gathering place for artists and musicians as well as a deep harbor for a fleet of pleasure vessels. The whole area is a center for many of the passenger schooners which offer weekly trips along the Maine coast.

One of the most striking *(continued on page 160)*

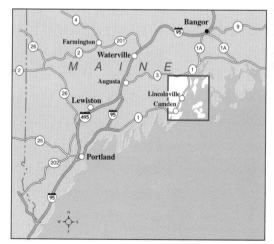

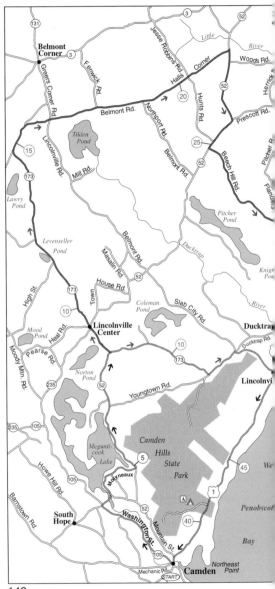

142

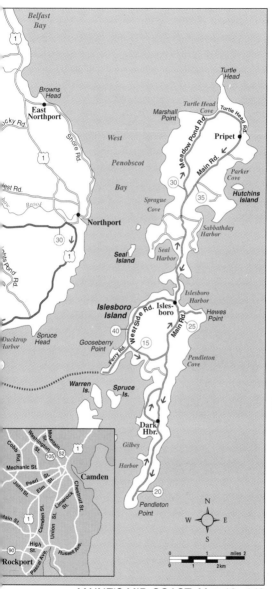

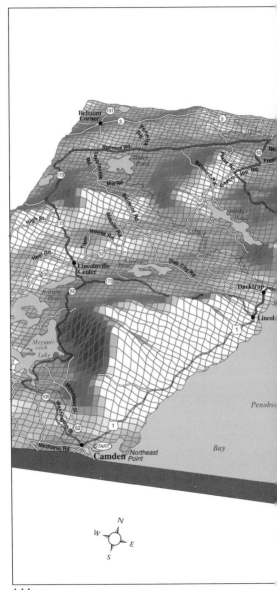

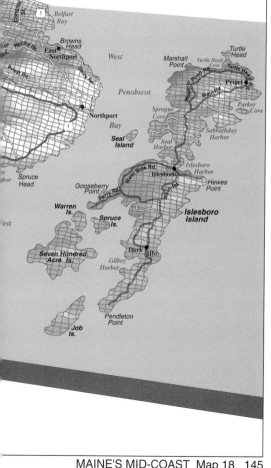

Belfast
Bay

Browns
Head

East
Northport

West

Penobscot

Northport

Bay

Seal
Island

Spruce
Head

Gooseberry
Point

Warren
Is.

Spruce
Is.

Seven Hundred
Acre Is.

Job
Is.

Gilbey
Harbor

Pendleton
Point

Dark Hbr.

Islesboro
Island

Hewes
Point

Islesboro
Harbor

Islesboro

West Side Rd.

Seal
Harbor

Sprague
Cove

Sabbathday
Harbor

Marshall
Point

Turtle Head
Cove

Turtle
Head

Pripet

Parker
Cove

Ferry Rd.

Main Rd.

Moccy V. Pond Rd.

Main Rd.

Priest Rd.

Rocky Rd.

Shore Rd.

Compres St.

ISLEBORO ISLAND

48.0 miles

0   Start in Camden at the intersection of Rt. 1 and Washington St.; head west on Wash. St.

0.5   Continue straight at the three-way stop to stay on Washington St.

2.7   **Turn right on Molyneaux Rd. after pond** (unmarked).

3.2   **Turn left.**

4.7   Megunticook Lake Beach.

4.9   **Turn left on Rt. 52.**

6.8   **Bear left to stay on Rt. 52.**

8.4   **Turn right on Rt. 173.**

13.5   Continue straight across Rt. 1 towards Isleboro Ferry.
Note: For the shortest ride, turn right onto Rt. 1 South. Camden is 6.1 miles on the right.

13.6   Ferry landing. Take ferry to Isleboro Island. Go straight after departing the ferry.

14.7   **Turn right at sign for Dark Harbor.**

15.7   **Turn right toward Dark Harbor.**
Note: If you turn left here to go to the northern end of the island, you'll cut 8.5 miles off the ride.

17.7   Dark Harbor. Continue straight.

20.1   Pendleton Point. **Turn around point.**

21.3   **Turn left.** The Blue Heron restaurant is on the right after turn.

21.6   Keep right.

21.8   Continue straight to stay on this road.

23.1   **Turn left.**

25.3   **Turn right, just past small baseball field.**

25.9   **Turn around point.**

26.5   **Turn right.**

26.7   **Keep right;** Isleboro Historical Society on left.

29.5   **Bear left.**

35.6   **Turn left.**

38.4   **Turn right just past the Historical Society.**

(continued on right)

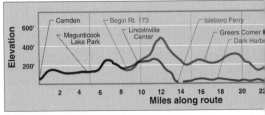

NORTHPORT

41.5 miles

0   Start in Camden at the intersection of Rt. 1 and Washington St.; head west on Washington St.; follow Isleboro Route to milepost 8.4.

8.4   **Turn right on Rt. 173.**

8.5   **Turn left on Rt 173 N. toward Lincolnville Center.**

9.4   Lincolnville Center; continue straight.

14.9   **Turn right on Belfast Union Rd.**

15.7   **Turn right uphill, farmhouse on left.**

16.4   Intersection with Greers Corner Rd./ Lincolnville Rd.; school on left.; continue straight.

19.5   Intersection with Northport Rd.; stay left.

20.6   Intersection with Hunts Rd.; continue straight.

22.1   **Turn right on Rt. 52 S.**

24.1   **Turn right to stay on Rt. 52 S. at intersection with Prescott Rd.**

25.2   **Turn left** (sign on tree may mark Beech Hill Rd).

30.3   **Turn right on Rt. 1.**

35.3   Continue straight at intersection with road to Isleboro ferry.

41.5   End in Camden at intersection with Washington St.

Northport (continued)

40.6   **Turn right towards ferry landing.**

41.7   Ferry landing. Go straight after departing the ferry. Turn left on Rt. 1 South.

48.0   End in Camden at the intersection of Rt. 1 and Washington St.

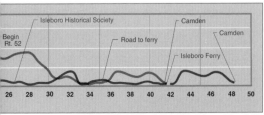

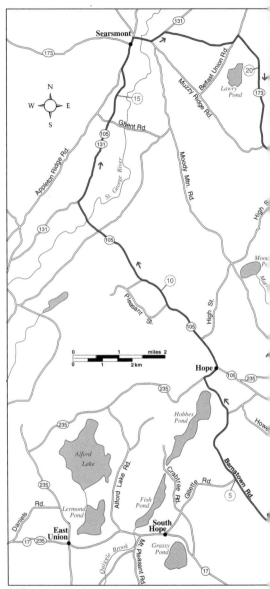

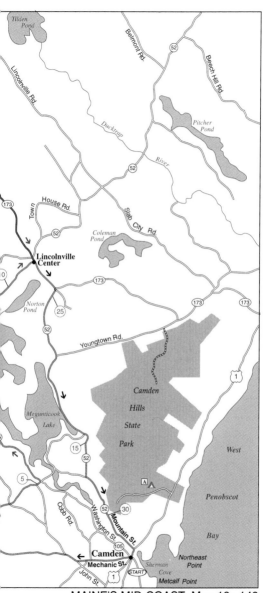

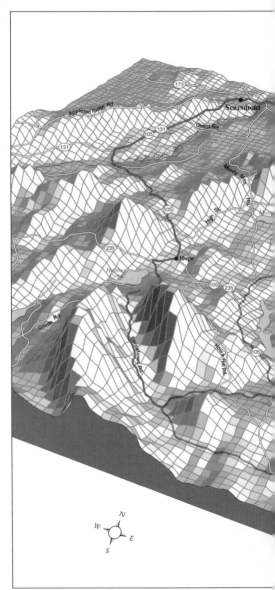

Appleton Ridge Rd.

173

Scarsmont

Ghent Rd.

131

105

131

Mt. George Rd.

Moody Mtn. Rd.

105

High St.

Moo

235

Hope

Hobbes
Pond

105 235

Gillette Rd.

Barnstown Rd.

Howe Hill Rd.

105

N
W   E
S

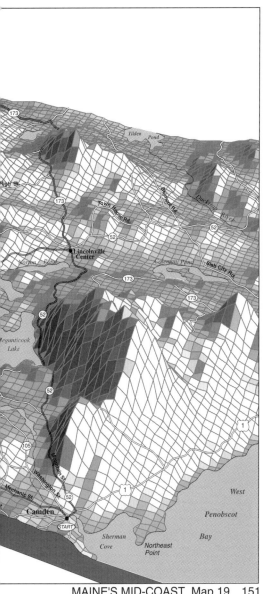

MEGUNTICOOK LAKE

17.8 miles

0   Start in Camden at the intersection of Rt. 1 and Washington St.; head west on Washington St.

0.1   Turn left on Mechanic St. (may be unmarked).

1.5   Turn right at sign for Camden Snow Bowl.

3.5   Turn right at small grassy island; view of pond of ski area on left.

4.5   Keep left at 'Y' intersection.

5.2   Turn left on Rt. 105 W.

7.8   Turn right on Rt. 235 N. toward Lincolnville Center.

10.8   Turn right on Rt. 173; Lincolnville Center.

11.6   Turn right on Rt. 52 S. towards Camden.

17.7   Turn right on Rt. 1 S. in Camden.

17.8   End in Camden at the interesection of Rt. 1 and Washington St.

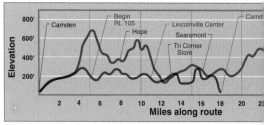

SEARSMONT

31.0 miles

Start in Camden at the intersection of Rt. 1 and Washington St.; head west on Washington St.

.1   **Turn left on Mechanic St.** (may be unmarked).

.5   **Turn right at sign for Camden Snow Bowl.**

.5   **Bear left at the 'Y' intersection.** Ski area on left after turn.

.5   **Turn right;** cemetery on right.

.0   **Turn left on Rt. 105;** Hope General Store.

2.7   **Turn right on Rt. 131 N.;** Tri Corner Store on left.

6.3   Keep right on Rt. 131 N.; town of Searsmont.

7.0   **Turn right on Rt. 173 toward Lincolnville.**

8.8   Keep right, continuing on Rt. 173 S.

1.6   Lake on right.

4.0   Lincolnville Center; continue straight on Rts. 52/173.

4.8   **Turn right on Rt. 52 S. toward Camden.**

0.9   **Turn right on Rt. 1 S. in Camden.**

1.0   End in Camden at the intersection of Rt. 1 and Washington St.

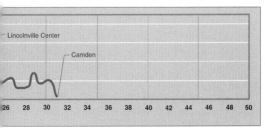

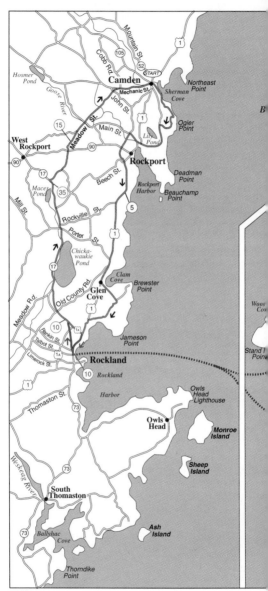

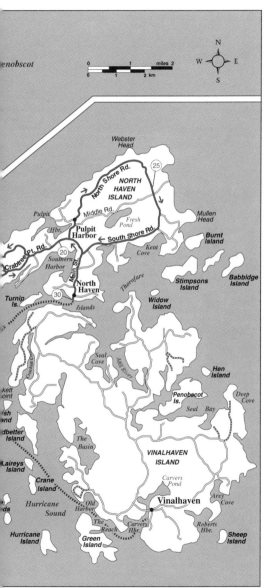

NORTH HAVEN ISLAND

Webster Head

North Shore Rd.

(25)

Middle Rd.

Fresh Pond

Pulpit Hbr.

Pulpit Harbor

Mullen Head

Crabtree Pt. Rd.

Southern Harbor

South Shore Rd.

Kent Cove

Burnt Island

(20)

Main St.

North Haven

Thorofare

Stimpsons Island

Babbidge Island

Turnip Is.

(30)

Islands

Widow Island

Seal Cove

Mill River

Hen Island

Penobscot Is.

Seal Bay

Deep Cove

kett oint

ish and

dbetter Island

Laireys Island

The Basin

VINALHAVEN ISLAND

Crane Island

Hurricane Sound

Old Harbor

Carvers Pond

Areys Cove

Vinalhaven

ds

The Reach

Carvers Hbr.

Roberts Hbr.

Hurricane Island

Green Island

Sheep Island

enobscot

N
W   E
S

miles   1   2
0
0   1   2 km

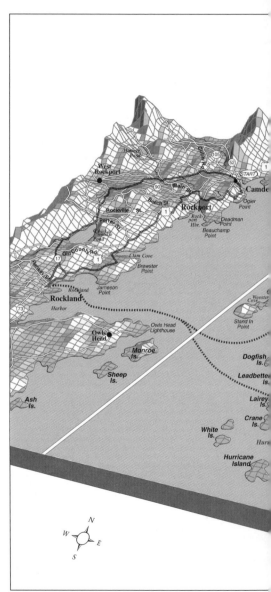

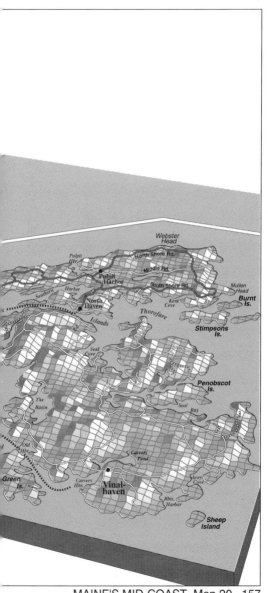

Webster
Head

Pulpit
Hbr.

North Shore Rd.

Middle Rd.

**Pulpit
Harbor**

South Shore Rd.

Mullen
Head

Southern

Harbor

Kent
Cove

**Burnt
Is.**

**North
Haven**

Islands

Thorofare

**Stimpsons
Is.**

*Seal
Cove*

**Penobscot
Is.**

*The
Basin*

Seal Bay

*Old
Hbr.*

*Carvers
Pond*

**Green
Is.**

*Carvers
Hbr.*

**Vinal-
haven**

*Arey
Cove*

*Rbts.
Harbor*

**Sheep
Island**

ROCKLAND

18.0 miles

0	Start in Camden at the intersection of Rt. 1 and Washington St.; head north on Rt. 1.
0.1	**Turn right on Bayview St.**
1.8	**Turn left on Chestnut St.**
2.9	Rockland. Keep left.
3.0	**Bear right then turn left across cement bridge.**
3.7	**Turn left on Rt. 1 S.**
7.0	**Turn left at bottom of the hill on Warrington Rd.**
8.2	Keep right at Samoset Resort.
8.7	**Turn left on Rt. 1.**
9.1	**Turn right on Rt. 1A.**
9.7	Continue straight on Rt. 17.
10.8	Chickawaukie Pond.
13.8	**Turn right on Meadow St.** (first paved road on the right).
14.8	Continue straight across Rt. 90.
15.7	Continue straight at intersection.
16.8	Continue straight at intersection.
16.9	**Turn right on Mechanic St.** (unmarked).
17.9	**Turn left at blinking red light.**
18.0	End in Camden at intersection of Washington St. and Rt. 1.

North Haven Island *(continued)*

30.9	**Turn left to stay on Rt. 17.**
32.0	Chickawaukie Pond.
35.0	**Turn right on Meadow St.** (first paved road on the right).
36.0	Continue straight across Rt. 90.
36.9	Continue straight.
38.0	Continue straight at stop sign.
38.1	**Turn right on Mechanic St.** (unmarked).
39.1	**Turn left at red light.**
39.2	End in Camden at intersection of Washington St. and Rt. 1.

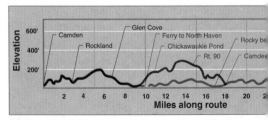

NORTH HAVEN ISLAND

39.2 miles

0 Start in Camden at the intersection of Rt. 1
and Washington St.; head north on Rt. 1.;
follow Rockland route directions to mile 8.7.

8.7 **Bear right; Rt. 1 becomes one way; then
bear left;** stay on Rt. 1.

8.8 **Turn left on Talbot Ave.;** follow sign for
erry.

0.0 Board ferry; general store on right as
you disembark on North Haven Island.

0.1 **Turn right on the main road; turn left to
go uphill.**

0.2 **Turn left.**

0.3 **Turn right.**

1.5 **Bear left.**

2.1 **Turn left;** Grange Hall on right; Pulpit
Harbor Inn on left.
*Note: To cut off 8.7 miles continue
straight here and refer to mile 20.8 for
further route directions.*

3.6 **Turn right at the 'Y' intersection;** first
paved right.

3.9 **Turn left;** pavement ends here.

4.3 Pavement begins.

5.0 **Turn right on Crabtree Point Rd.;**

6.9 **Rocky beach; turn around point.**

20.8 **Turn left;** Pulpit Harbor Inn on left.

21.2 **Bear left** (not uphill).

21.4 **Turn right after bridge;** follow paved
North Shore Rd. around the eastern end
of the island; becomes South Shore Rd.

28.6 **Bear left to go back to town.**

30.0 **Turn right;** General Store on left; ferry
landing ahead.

30.1 **Turn right on Rt. 1 as you leave parking
lot in Rockland.**

30.2 **Turn left on Rt. 17.**

30.7 Continue straight on Rt. 17 W.

(continued on left)

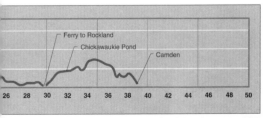

(continued from page 141)

topographic features of the area are the Camden Hills which rise almost 1400 ft. from the sea. Camden Hills State Park covers about 5000 acres of this formation, and offers camping areas and hiking trails. There is also a road to Mt. Battie's 900 ft. summit, from which you can enjoy wonderful panoramic views of Penobscot Bay, nearby coastal towns, and the rolling inland countryside.

It is a pleasure to get to and cycle on the two islands visited on these routes: Isleboro on day one, and North Haven on day two. The 25-minute ferry ride to Isleboro puts you on an island with gentle topography and miles of quiet roads. After sailing a little over an hour from Rockland, you'll arrive at North Haven Island, which has the same kind of quiet roads winding over an only slightly hillier landscape – one that yields many views over the water to surrounding islands and mainland. Vinalhaven is a third island that is accessible for day rides in this area, though it is perhaps not as picturesque as the others.

Inland from Camden you'll find many more miles of quiet, country roads. While days one and three combine inland routes with coastal and island roads, day two is entirely oriented to the interior. Rolling hills are blanketed by farms and forest, and the valleys are dotted with a number of lakes and ponds.

There is plenty of variety here in the combination of coastal, island, and inland riding. While we have laid out three days worth of cycling, it would be easy to spend a week or more exploring this beautiful region. In addition to cycling, certainly allow some time to experience the sea – hiking, tidepooling, beachcombing, sailing, and sea kayaking opportunities abound!

Around New England

In this chapter you will find information about accommodations, campgrounds, and points of interest. It is organized by regions corresponding to the sets of maps displayed in pages 25 to 160 in this book. The letters in boxes next to campground listings are keyed to identical symbols on the road maps for that region.

Lake Champlain

Chambers of Commerce/ Visitor Information Centers:
• Brandon Info. Center. Rt. 7, Box 267, Brandon, VT 05733.
• Addison County Chamber. (802) 388-7951. 2 Court St., Middlebury, VT 05753.

Accommodations:
Brandon.
• Contact Brandon Info. Center listed above.
Middlebury.
• Contact Addison County Chamber listed above.
Shelburne, VT 05482.
• Countryside Motel. 985-2839. Box 277.
• The Dutch Mill Motel. 985-8057. Rt. 7, 2031 Shelburne Rd.
• Red Carpet Inn. (800) 825-1882. 1961 ShelburneRd.
• Shelburne House. 985-8686. Harbor Rd.
• Shelburne Travelodge. 985-8037. 1907 Shelburne Rd.
• T-Bird Motel. 985-3663. 2062 Shelburne Rd.
• Yankee Doodle Motel. 985-8004. Rt. 7, 2027 Shelburne Rd.
Vergennes, VT 05491.
• Basin Harbor Club. (800) 622-4000. 600 Basin Harbor Rd.
• Chimney Point House. 759-2632. RD3, Box 248.
• Emerson's Guest House B&B. 877-3293. 82 Main St.
• New Haven Motor Inn. 877-2956. RR2, Box 188.
• The Strong House Inn. 877-3337. Rt. 22A.

Public Camping Facilities:
Brandon, VT 05733.
Ⓙ Branbury State Park. 247-5925. RR2, Box 2621.
Vergennes, VT 05491.
Ⓛ Button Bay State Park. 475-2377. RD3, Box 570.
Ⓘ DAR State Park. 759-2354. RD3, Box 214.
N. Ferrisburg, VT 05473
Ⓚ Mt. Philo State Park. 425-2390. RD1, Box 1049.

Private Camping Facilities:
Addison, VT 05491.
D Ten Acre Campground. 759-2662. RD3, Box 262.
Bristol, VT 05443.
C Elephant Mountain Camping Area. 453-3123. RD3,
    Box 850.
B Winona Recreation Area. 453-3439. RD2, Box 4680.
Brandon, VT 05733.
F Country Village Campground. 247-3333. RD2.
G Smoke Rise Family Campground. 247-6472.
New Haven, VT 05472.
A Rivers Bend Campsites. 388-9092. RD1.
Salisbury, VT 05679
E Lake Dunmore Kampersville. 352-4501.
Shelburne, VT 05482.
H Shelburne Camping Area. 985-2540. Rt.7.
Vergennes, VT 05491.
• Hillcrest Campground & Cottages. 475-2343. 877 B
    Basin Harbor Rd.

Points of Interest:
Addison.
• Chimney Point. Site of pre-1800 inn and tavern.
    Tavern and museum.
• John Strong DAR Mansion.
Basin Harbor.
• Lake Champlain Maritime Museum. 475-2317.
Ferrisburg.
• Rokeby Museum. Home of Rowland E. Robinson,
    Vermont writer. Furnished with 18th & 19th
    century antiques and decorative arts. 877-3406.
Middlebury.
• Sheldon Museum. Three-story 19th century furnished
    home.
• Vermont Folklife Center.
Orwell.
• Mt. Independence. Site of Revolutionary War
    fortifications. Over three miles of trails.
Shelburne.
• Shelburne Farms. Former estate of railroad magnate
    William Seward Webb. Active dairy farm, bakery,
    cheese-making. Visitor Center and cheese shop.
Weybridge.
• Univ. of Vermont Morgan Horse Farm.

Fair Haven

Chambers of Commerce/ Visitor Information Centers:
• Fair Haven Chamber. 265-4924. Box 8, Fair Haven,
    VT 05743.

Accommodations:
Fair Haven, VT 05735.
• Fair Haven Inn. 265-4907. 5 Adams St.
• Maplewood Inn. 265-8039. Rt. 22A South.
• Vermont Maple Inn. 265-8383. 12 W. Park Pl.
Lake Bomoseen, VT 05732.
• Edgewater Motor Lodge. 468-5251. Rt. 30.
• Prospect House & Bomoseen Golf Club. 468-5581.
    Rt. 30.

Poultney/East Poultney.
- Lake St. Catherine Inn. 287-9347. Box 129V, Poultney, VT 05764.
- Stoneybridge Inn. 287-9849. Rt. 30, Poultney, VT 05764.
- Eagle Tavern on the Green. 287-9498. Box 587, East Poultney, VT 05741

Public Camping Facilities:
Fair Haven, VT 05743.
G Bomoseen State Park. 265-4242. RR1, Box 2620.
H Half Moon State Park. 273-2848. RR1, Box 2730.
Poultney, VT 05764.
I Lake St. Catherine State Park. 287-9158. RD2, Box 230.

Private Camping Facilities:
Danby.
F Otter Creek Campground. 362-1847.
Hubbardton.
B Big D Camp Grounds. 273-2021.
North Clarendon.
E Iroquois Land Family Camping. 773-2832.
Pittsford.
C Smoke Rise Family Campground. 247-6472.
Sudbury.
D Andy's Camp Grounds. 273-2751.
West Castleton.
A Lake Bomoseen Campground. 273-2061.

Points of Interest:
Brandon.
- Maple-cutting mills led to prosperity of this birthplace of Stephen Douglas.
Castleton.
- Federal and Greek Revival architecture.
Danby.
- Marble quarry village featuring wood frame gable roofed residences.
East Hubbardton.
- The Hubbardton Battlefield and Museum is seven miles off U.S. 4.
Pittsford.
- Pittsford Green. Features a wide variety of architectural styles surrounding a triangular village green.
- The New England Maple Museum. 483-9414.
Poultney.
- This was a stage stop and later a prominent slate center.
Rutland.
- The arrival of the railroad and a boom in the marble industry caused a tripling of the population between 1850 and 1880. Marble was used extensively in construction of many architecturally significant buildings.
- Norman Rockwell Museum. 773-6095.
Tinmouth.
- The 16 significant structures include Stick style, Federal, Greek Revival, and Italianate.
- The main street (Rt. 7) includes a full range of 19th century residential styles with few intrusions.

Connecticut River Valley

Chambers of Commerce/ Visitor Information Centers:
- Ludlow Chamber. (802) 228-5318. 196 Main St., Box 333, Ludlow, VT 05149.
- Quechee Chamber. 295-7900. Box 106, Quechee, VT 05059.
- Springfield Chamber. 885-2779. Clinton St., Springfield, VT 05156.
- Windsor Area Chamber. 674-5910. 54 Main St., Box 5, Windsor, VT 05089.
- Woodstock Chamber. 457-3555. Box 486, Woodstock, VT 05091.

Accommodations:
Ascutney, VT 05030.
- Yankee Village Motel. 674-6010. Rt. 5, Box 84.

Grafton, VT 05146.
- The Hayes House. 843-2461. Bear Hill Rd.
- The Inn at Woodchuck Hill Farm. 843-2398. Middletown Rd.
- The Old Tavern at Grafton. 843-2231. Main St. & Townsend Rd.

Ludlow.
- Contact Ludlow Chamber listed above.

Plymouth, VT 05056.
- Farmbrook Motel. 672-3621. Rt. 100A.
- Hawk Inn & Mountain Resort. 672-3811. Box 64.
- Salt Ash Inn. 672-5214. Jct. Rts. 100 & 100A.
- Stoney Creek. 672-5214. HCR 70, Box 48A.

Quechee.
- Contact Quechee Chamber listed above.

Springfield.
- Contact Springfield Chamber listed above.

Windsor, VT 05089.
- Country Vista Motor Lodge. 674-5565. Box 395.
- The Gingerbread House. 674-2322. 5 Court St.
- Juniper Hill Inn. 674-5273. Juniper Hill Rd.

Woodstock.
- Contact Woodstock Chamber listed above.

Public Camping Facilities:
Plymouth, VT 05056.
🄹 Coolidge State Park. 672-3612. HCR70, Box 105.
White River Jct., VT 05001.
🄻 Quechee Gorge State Park. 295-2290. White River Jct.
Windsor, VT 05089.
🄺 Ascutney State Park. 674-2060. HCR71, Box 186.

Private Camping Facilities:
Andover.
🄷 Horseshoe Acres. 875-2960.
Ludlow.
🄰 Hideaway Campgrounds. 228-8800.
🄲 Meadow Brook Farm. 226-7755.
Plymouth.
🄱 Plymouth Village Campground. 672-3708.
Springfield.
🄶 Tree Farm Campground. 885-2889.
🄵 Hidden Valley Campground. 886-2497.
Weathersfield Center.
🄳 Caton Place Campground. 226-7767.
🄴 Crown Point Camping Area. 263-5555.
164

Points of Interest:
Chester Point.
• Stone Village District has a number of stone buildings and ashlar construction.
Ludlow.
• Black River Academy Historical Museum. 228-5050.
Plymouth.
• Birthplace of Calvin Coolidge, 30th President. Several buildings and a visitor's center operated by Vermont Div. of Historic Preservation.
Saxtons River.
• This historic district includes Federal, Greek Revival, Italianate, Queen Anne and Colonial Revival architectural styles.
South Woodstock.
• Includes Federal and Greek Revival structures.
Springfield.
• Art and Historical Society. 885-2415. 9 Elm Hill.
• The Eureka Schoolhouse. This is the oldest school in Vermont (1785).
Woodstock.
• Site of nation's first ski resort features a tree-shaded elliptical green, the Dana House museum and the Ottauquechee DAR house (1807).
• Billings Farm and Museum. 457-2355.
• Woodstock Historical Society. 457-1822.

Heart of Vermont

Chambers of Commerce/ Visitor Information Centers:
• Central Vermont Chamber of Commerce. (802) 229-5711. Box 336, Barre, VT 05641.

Accommodations:
Stowe.
• Contact Stowe Area Assoc. 800-24-STOWE. Box 1320, Stowe, VT 05672.
Waterbury, VT 05676.
• Grünberg Haus. 244-7726. RR2, Box 1595.
• Holiday Inn. 244-7822. Exit 10, I-89 & Rt. 100N.
• Inn at Blush Hill. 244-5056. 18 N. Main St.
• The Old Stagecoach Inn. 244-5056. 18 N. Main St.
• Thatcher Brook Inn. 244-5911. RD2, Box 62.

Public Camping Facilities:
Waterbury, VT 05676.
Ⓐ Little River State Park. 244-7103. RD1, Box 1150.

Private Camping Facilities:
Moscow.
Ⓑ Gold Brook Campground. 253-7683.

Points of Interest:
Montpelier.
• State House. Chosen as the Capital in 1808.
• The Vermont Museum. 828-2291. 109 State St.
Waterbury.
• Ben & Jerry's Ice Cream Factory Tours. Rt. 100.
• Village of Waterbury has architecture ranging from Federal to Queen Anne styles.
• Mill Village, with its Greek Revival and Colonial Revival structures embellish evidence of small-scale 19th century manufacturing.

Stowe

Accommodations:
Stowe.
• Contact Stowe Area Assoc. 800-24-STOWE. Box
    1320, Stowe, VT 05672.

Public Camping Facilities:
Lake Elmore, VT 05657.
◧ Elmore State Park. 888-2982. Box 93.

Private Camping Facilities:
Morrisville.
◧ Mountain View Cottages and Campground. 796-3733.
Moscow.
◧ Gold Brook Campground. 253-7683.

Points of Interest:
Morrisville.
• Noyes House Museum. 19th century exhibits of local
    and regional history. 888-5605.
• The Hearthstone Stove Factory. Handcrafted
    woodburning stoves, tours available. 888-4568.
Stowe.
• Bloody Brook School House. Restored 1845 one-room
    schoolhouse. 253-7227.
• The Gondola. Takes you up Mt. Mansfield.
• Stowe Village. One of Vermont's oldest resorts.

Cape Islands

Chambers of Commerce/ Visitor Information Centers:
• Martha's Vineyard Chamber. 508) 693-0085. Beach
    Rd., Box 1698, Vineyard Haven, MA 02568.
• Nantucket Chamber. 228-1700. Box SG, Nantucket
    Island, MA 02554.

Accommodations:
Martha's Vineyard.
• Contact Chamber listed above or the following reserva-
    tion services:
• Accommodations Plus. 693-6505. RFD273, Edgar-
    town, MA 02539.
• Dukes Co. Reservations Service. 693-6505. Box 1522,
    Oak Bluffs, MA 02557.
• Houseguests Cape Cod and the Islands. 896-7053.
    Box 1881, Orleans, MA 02653.
• Martha's Vineyard & Nantucket Reservations. 693-
    7200. Box 1322, Vineyard Haven, MA 02568.
• Martha's Vineyard Properties. (800) 336-4820. Box
    4388, Vineyard Haven, MA 02568.
Nantucket.
• Contact Chamber listed above or the following reserva-
    tion services:
• Martha's Vineyard & Nantucket Reservations. 693-
    7200. Box 1322, Vineyard Haven, MA 02568.
• Houseguests Cape Cod and the Islands. 896-7053.
    Box 1881, Orleans, MA 02653.

Private Camping Facilities:
Martha's Vineyard.
- **Ⓐ** Martha's Vineyard Family Campground. 693-3772. Edgartown Rd. Box 1557, Vineyard Haven.
- **Ⓑ** Webb's Camping Area. 693-0233. RFD2, Box 100, Vineyard Haven.

Points of Interest:
Martha's Vineyard.
- Flying Horses Carousel. Oldest carousel in U.S resides in Oak Bluffs.
- Vincent House. Oldest (1672) house on the island.
- Olde School House Museum. Lots of Revolutionary and whaling artifacts here. 627-4440.
- Dukes Co. Historical Society Museum. School & Cooke Sts., Edgartown. 627-4440.

Nantucket.
- Whaling Museum. 228-1894. Broad St.
- Old Mill. Built in 1746 and still mills corn with the wind's power. 228-1894.
- 1800 House. Typical architectural style for 19th century Nantucket house. 228-1894.
- Old North Church. Great views from tower. Centre St.

Maine

Chambers of Commerce/ Visitor Information Centers:
- Camden/Lincolnville/Rockport Chamber. (207) 236-4404. Box 919, Camden, ME 04843.
- Thomaston Chamber. 354-2326. Box 10 Thomaston, ME 04861.
- Rockland Chamber. 596-0376. Box 508, Harbor Park, ME 04841.

Accommodations:
Camden.
- Contact Chamber listed above.
Glen Cove, ME 04846.
- Glen Cove Motel. 594-4062. Rt. 1.
- The Ledges Motor Court. 594-8944.
- Sea View Motel. 594-8479. Rt. 1.
- Strawberry Hill Motor Court. 594-5462. Rt.1.
Hope, ME 04847.
- Blanchard Bed & Breakfast. 763-3785. Hatchet Mountain Rd.
Isleboro.
- Dark Harbor House Inn. 734-6669.
- Isleboro Inn Dark Harbor. 734-2222.
- Moss Inn. 734-6410.
Lincolnville.
- Contact Chamber listed above.
North Haven, ME 04853.
- Pulpit Harbor Inn. 867-2219. Crabtree Point Rd.
Northport, ME 04915.
- Bayside Inn. 338-1777. Bayside Rd.
- Green Woods Cabins. 338-3187.
- Northport Motel. 338-3018. Rt. 1.
- Oxbow Motel. 338-3018. Rt. 1.

Rockland, ME 04841.
- Navigator Motor Inn. 594-2131. 520 Main St.
- Rockland Motel. 594-5471. Rt. 1.
- Trade Winds Motor Inn. 596-6661. 303 Maine St.

Rockport.
- Contact Chamber listed above.

Searsmont, ME 04973.
- Camp Wah-Nah-Gee-Sha. 338-3829.

South Thomaston, ME 04858.
- Craignair Inn. 594-7644. Clark Island Rd.
- Weskeag Inn. 596-6676. Rt. 73.

Sprucehead, ME 04859.
- Island View Ocean Front Cottages. 594-7527. Patten Point Rd.
- The Off-Island Store & Motel. 594-7475.

Vinalhaven, ME 04863.
- Fox Island Inn. 863-2122. Carver St.
- Libby House B & B. 863-4696. Water St.
- Morning Glory B & B. 863-2051.
- Tidewater Motel. 863-4618. Main St.

Public Camping Facilities:
Camden.
A Camden Hills State Park.

Private Camping Facilities:
Camden.
- Camden Campground. 236-2478.

Lincolnville Beach, ME 04849.
- Old Massachusetts Homestead. 789-5135. Rt.1.

Rockport, ME 04841.
- Megunticook by the Sea Campground. 594-2428. Rt.1.
- Roberts Roost Campground. 236-2498. Rt. 90.

South Thomaston, ME 04841.
- Lobster Buoy Campsite. 594-7546. Watermans Beach Rd.

Points of Interest:
Camden.
- Old Conway House Complex. An 18th century farmhouse with a variety of antiques.

Rockland.
- William A. Farnsworth Library, Art Museum and Homestead. Lots of American paintings are displayed.

Cycling Information

Bicycle riding in the New England countryside is fun, and will be safer when common sense and basic safety rules are followed. Knowing the rules of the road, developing good riding skills, maintaining a properly equipped bicycle, and matching a route to your fitness and skill level will add up to many miles of pleasurable cycle touring.

Safety tips

In general:
- **Be predictable.** Ride so drivers can see you and predict your movements. The rules in the state driver's manual also apply to bicyclists.
- **Be alert.** Ride defensively and expect the unexpected. No matter who is at fault in an accident, the bicyclist loses.
- **Be equipped.** You will ride easier and safer if you and your bike have proper equipment.
- **Wear a helmet.** A hard shell helmet, meeting ANSI or Snell performance standards, is an essential element in your safety program.

Country riding:
- Ride single file and keep to the right when vehicles are approaching from behind and on sections of road with poor visibility.
- Slow down for gravel, sand, wet leaves, potholes, and other poor pavement conditions.
- Watch for dogs — dismount and place your bike between you and the dog if necessary.
- Be prepared for the air turbulence caused by fast moving vehicles or large trucks.
- Treat railroad crossings with respect. Cross perpendicular to the tracks and assure yourself that it is clear and safe before making the crossing.
- Stop where you are visible, or pull well off the road; avoid stopping on the tops of hills and at curves with blind approaches.
- Ride during daylight hours and wear brightly colored clothing.

Bicycle maintenance

Your bicycle requires periodic inspection and maintenance to keep it running reliably and safely. Several good books are available at bike shops, bookstores, and libraries, and bicycle maintenance and repair classes are sometimes offered through the cities and schools.

Here are just a few maintenance pointers:

- Regularly lubricate your bike with the correct type of lubricant.
- Brakes should be checked and adjusted if necessary. Brake shoes should be about one-eighth inch from the rim.
- The chain should be lubricated and clean, and the gears properly adjusted.
- Tires should be fully inflated.
- The frame and attachments should be tight.
- Seat and handlebars should be adjusted correctly for you.

Equipment

Since most of the routes in this book are located in very rural settings, it is wise to carry at least a basic tool kit with you on your excursions. Your tool kit should include at least the following items:
- tire repair kit
- tire irons
- pump
- tube valve tool (if not part of valve cap)
- small crescent wrench
- screwdriver

In addition, it may be useful to have:
- spoke wrench
- pliers
- oil
- tape
- allen wrenches
- freewheel remover

Spare parts that can come in handy include:
- cables for derailleur and brakes
- tube
- brake shoes (2)
- spokes (3)

Almost all of these tools and parts will fit into a small seat or handlebar bag, and with them you can tackle just about any problem not requiring a bicycle shop or expert attention.

Clothing

Wearing the right clothes and being prepared for adverse weather conditions will allow you to pedal merrily through varying weather patterns. Consider including these items in your riding wardrobe:

- a hat (in addition to your helmet)
- rain jacket or cape
- rain pants
- pant leg clips
- riding gloves
- sunglasses
- thermal tights and shirt
- riding shorts
- additional layers of clothing
- sun screen and insect repellent
- first aid kit
- pocket knife

Additional items for camping

Bicycle:
- front and/or rear racks and paniers

Clothes:
- long sleeved T-shirt
- bathing suit
- extra socks and underwear
- thongs or sandals
- long pants
- wool socks

Personal:
- towel
- toilet paper
- notebook
- camera and film
- needle and thread
- moleskin
- safety pins
- a good book

Camping:
- tent or tarp and groundcloth
- sleeping bag and pad
- small stove and fuel
- cooking kit, eating utensils, and knife
- biodegradable soap and pot scrubber
- waterproof matches
- flashlight and candle
- nylon cord
- plastic bags and litterbags
- food basics (salt, pepper, spices, etc.)

Fitness

Cycling in New England is going to involve some physical effort. Some routes will require more from you than others, but all will have their challenges – either in their length, their hilliness, or in the weather conditions you'll encounter. If you are prepared, both mentaly and physically, you'll enjoy your trip from the first day. Here are a couple of ways to prepare yourself physically.

1. Ride your bike before you go. Put together a trip plan and note how long the routes are – and what kind of terrain they follow. Then, on weekends and evenings before leaving, work up to rides of that distance and hilliness. If you are going to be camping, load some weight into your paniers and tackle some challenging hills. One of the advantages to this approach is the confidence you'll develop in your abilities.

2. Break in as you go. You still need to do a little riding before you go, but it is possible to plan a trip that starts easy and takes on more challenges along the way. You might take one or two short day trips and then embark on a several day loop. It takes a few days to build your stamina, and if you allow yourself to do it slowly, it will pay off in fewer sore muscles.

One of the most pleasant side effects of cycle touring is that you'll come home feeling fit and healthy. It is often suggested that you get a physical examination and discuss your fitness status with your doctor before taking on a new physical challenge like a bicycle tour. For the casual day-tripper and serious biker alike, cycling should not be debilitating. Pace yourself,enjoy your activity,and plan your trip to accommodate your fitness level.

More Cycling Guides from Terragraphics

Touring the Washington, D.C. Area by Bicycle

From the pastoral eastern shore of the Chesapeake Bay to the forested slopes of the Blue Ridge Mountains, the countryside surrounding our nation's capital offers cyclists a wide variety of terrain and landscapes. Thirty-one loop rides are described in detail, and hundreds of miles of good cycling roads are shown. You'll find routes that explore D.C.'s monuments, some off-road urban trails, and even mountain parkways.

$10.95   ISBN 0-944376-07-X

Touring the San Francisco Bay Area by Bicycle

This book offers cyclists 34 rides in the region. Along with these selected loops, maps show hundreds of miles of good cycling roads for an area stretching from northern Marin County all the way to Santa Cruz. The routes included are as varied as the topography and weather of the Bay Area.

$10.95   ISBN 0-944376-05-3

Touring California's Wine Country by Bicycle

These California regions are known worldwide for the quality and variety of their wines. The 34 routes in this guidebook take into account wine tasting opportunities, enjoying the countryside, and getting a good workout. Features rides in Napa, Sonoma, Sierra foothill, Central Valley, and Coast regions.

$10.95   ISBN 0-944376-06-1

(continued)

Touring the Islands
Bicycling in the San Juan, Gulf and Vancouver Islands

This island group annually attracts thousands of cyclists – and for good reason. Country roads, spectacular scenery, ferry rides, and the easy-going atmosphere add up to a great cycling vacation. Twelve islands and the northwest Olympic Peninsula can accommodate from a one-day to a multi-week trip over a variety of terrain.

$10.95   ISBN 0-944376-01-0

Touring Seattle by Bicycle

Thirty-three rides covering a large portion of the Puget Sound area are included. Routes range in character from downtown urban to island farmland. A variety of ride lengths and topography makes this book useful to both novice and expert cyclists. Seattle area riders made this book a regional bestseller in 1989, and will find it a valuable tool for years to come.

$10.95   ISBN 0-944376-02-9

Terragraphics books are distributed by
Ten Speed Press.

Ask for them at your favorite bookstore

-or-

Order direct from Ten Speed Press. Please include $1.25 shipping and handling for the first book, and 50 cents for each additional book. California residents include local sales tax. Write for our free complete catalog of over 400 books and tapes.

TEN SPEED PRESS
Box 7123
Berkeley, California 94707
(800) 841-BOOK